My Life Is a Weapon

MY LIFE IS A WEAPON

A Modern History of Suicide Bombing

C H R I S T O P H   R E U T E R

Translated by Helena Ragg-Kirkby

PRINCETON UNIVERSITY PRESS • PRINCETON AND OXFORD

First published in 2002 as *Mein Leben ist eine Waffe* by C. Bertelsmann Verlag, an imprint of C. Bertelsmann Verlag, Munich, of the Verlagsgruppe Random House GmBH, and copyright © 2002 by C. Bertelsmann Verlag, Munich, Germany

English-language translation and abridgment are copyright © 2004 by Princeton University Press
Published by Princeton University Press, 41 William Street, Princeton, New Jersey 08540
In the United Kingdom: Princeton University Press, 3 Market Place, Woodstock, Oxfordshire OX20 1SY

Second printing, and first paperback printing, 2006
Paperback ISBN-13: 978-0-691-12615-9
Paperback ISBN-10: 0-691-12615-1

The Library of Congress has cataloged the cloth edition of this book as follows

Reuter, Christoph.
[Mein Leben ist eine Waffe. English]
My life is a weapon : a modern history of suicide bombing / Christoph Reuter; translated by Helena Ragg-Kirkby.
p.   cm.
Includes index.
ISBN 0-691-11759-4 (alk. paper)
1. Violence—Religious aspects—Islam.   2. Suicide bombers.   3. Martyrdom—Islam.   4. Islam and politics.   5. Arab-Israeli conflict.   I. Title.
BP190.5.VR4813 2004   2003069321
303.6'25—dc22

British Library Cataloging-in-Publication Data is available

This book has been composed in Sabon

Printed on acid-free paper. ∞

pup.princeton.edu

Printed in the United States of America

3   5   7   9   10   8   6   4

For Thomas Dreger (1965–2002)

Contents

CONTENTS

The Power of the Powerless,
the Powerlessness of the Powerful

You will notice that the plane will stop, then will start to fly again.
This is the hour in which you will meet God.
—Extract from the spiritual "instruction manual" for the suicide attack on the World
Trade Center, found in Muhammad Atta's briefcase

In the matter of courage (a morally neutral virtue):
whatever may be said of the perpetrators of Tuesday's slaughter,
they were not cowards.
—Susan Sontag

In the mid-1990s, when I began my research on suicide bombers, first in Israel and, later in Lebanon and Iran, they were a rare phenomenon. They were a part of the Middle Eastern terrorism scene—noticed only occasionally, and attributed to Islamic fundamentalism, by the West—although in fact no one knew much about who was committing these attacks and what motivated them. The name of al-Qaeda was known, at most, to Afghanistan experts. For us, there is something unnerving, something disturbing, about the notion that human beings would sacrifice their own lives in order to kill others, in the belief that their lives have value only as a weapon. In more remote areas—in Lebanon, in Israel—this is how it has always been: but not in the great cities of Europe or in the United States of America. It didn't affect us—or so we thought. We barely noticed that the explosions of these human bombs had reached epidemic proportions, and that the tactic had made its way to Sri Lanka in 1987 (long before it reached as far as Israel), or that, by the 1990s, it had arrived in Turkey, Kashmir, and Chechnya.

By the summer of 2003, suicide bombers had changed the world. The "end of history," hailed by winners of the Cold War, now appears in reality to have been merely the end of the old rules. On September 11, 2001, four attacks by nineteen suicide bombers, armed with nothing more lethal than a couple of box-cutters, suddenly forced America to start waging a new type of world war. As this is being written, George W. Bush's "war on terror" has toppled regimes in Afghanistan and Iraq; has deeply divided America from many of its Western allies; has enflamed anti-American prejudice in the Islamic world—and no one can say how it will end. To this date, the real enemy—the followers of Osama bin Laden, trained in suicide and murder, and embodying his nihilistic version of the ideology of a jihad bent on destroying everything—remains undefeated, as we see by the unending string of new attacks in such places as Casablanca, Riyadh, Mombasa, Karachi, Indonesia, Tunisia. Indeed, here is an opponent who cannot be defeated by superior military force; it has moved outside all the conventional rules of power and war in which we have always trusted.

"Cowardly" is how the early commentators, in their initial helplessness and horror, characterized the events of September 11; but they quickly came to see that the one thing these attacks most certainly were not was cowardly.

Suicide attacks affect us profoundly and powerfully. They remind us that there are people who consider their struggle—whatever the cause—to be more important than their own lives. They stir up fear in us; they pull the rug out from under our feet. For there is no way to retaliate against attackers who strike, not merely in order to kill people, but to die at the same stroke. They annihilate the entire logic of power, since no credible threat can be made against someone who has no desire to survive.

All our notions of security and our civilization have been based on this unspoken assumption, which we heretofore have believed to be self-evident. For example, consider that for airport security checks, up until now, the only precaution thought necessary was the matching of every piece of luggage with an on-board passenger, since, as everyone knew, nobody would think of blowing themselves up in midair. Or so we thought.

The presumption of individual rational self-interest and fear of death underlies the functioning of the market economy and the power of the state: suicide bombers cancel these out. Deterrence, punishment, and retaliation all become meaningless when faced with an aggressor who will impose the utmost penalty on himself at the very moment of his victory. The fear of death has long been the ultimate instrument of power wielded by the state and the priesthood, whether in the Christian church or in Islam: neither the state nor any other power can threaten us with anything worse than death. By the same token, the taboo against suicide has typically reinforced the power of religion, because of the conventional monotheistic belief that only God may decide who will live and who will die. But in the present case, we are faced with people in revolt not only against the state but also all other candidates for supreme authority, religious or secular. Suicide bombers simultaneously defy the ultimate sanction, rendering the mightiest power impotent. There is no sanction beyond that of death.

What we have experienced in recent years is the reinvention of a historical archetype that many political historians thought had long since disappeared: the martyr. Martyrs today are of incalculable propaganda value. They say to their own people: Follow our example—the cause is greater than our (and your) lives. And they say to the outside world: We fear humiliation more than we fear death, and, therefore, we have no fear of your well-trained and well-equipped armies, your high-tech arsenal. To the potential recruit for a suicide mission, the more powerless he may have felt before committing the attack, the more dramatically death will exalt him. After a life devoid of any previous significance, he now becomes a powerful ideal; his very name inspires fear. In his own person, he has realized Andy Warhol's dictum that everyone is allotted "fifteen minutes of fame."

Just as important as the killing is the dying that it makes it possible. The suicide attack that took place on August 12, 2001 (just a month before the attacks on New York), at the Wall Street Café in Shiriat Motzkin, a suburb of Haifa in northern Israel, seems in retrospect but a small, insignificant precursor of what was to come. It was barely reported at the time, and is now all but forgotten. On that day twenty-eight-year-old Muhammad Mahmoud Nassr, carrying enough explosives strapped to his waist to cause carnage, approached the waitress at the café bar, lifted his T-shirt, and asked her if she knew what "that" was. People started screaming and throwing chairs in his direction; everyone rushed outside. Muhammad Mahmoud Nassr, alone in the empty café, cried "Allahu akbar"—God is great—and then blew himself up: his torso was ripped apart, while his head landed on a table. It was a baffling and, fortunately for those in the café at the time, futile attack—and it was met with the same blank incomprehension that all such acts tended to evoke. The international and Israeli media passed over it, generally relieved that nobody had died—except the attacker, and that was *his* problem. Yet what looked like failure concealed an urgent hidden meaning: Look at how easily I could terrify you. And you are absolutely right to be afraid.

In its early centuries, Christendom was teeming with martyrs; early Islam was no stranger to them either. Even today, the city squares in the heart of Beirut and Damascus, for instance, are both called "Martyrs' Square." And today, in a modern world that knows only one, asymmetric superpower, the experience of total subjugation has returned. In an era when de facto suicide missions are routinely launched against political and military allies of the remaining superpower, the old ideals of martyrdom are gaining a new currency. The problem now, however, is that the ideal has been equipped with weapons and technologies of unprecedented destructive power.

Two thousand years ago, there were already certain groups who went into battle with the specific goal of dying, among these the Jewish Sicarians in the Imperial Roman world. Later, in the medieval Crusades, the assassins appeared; and such fighters took part in the Muslim revolts in the eighteenth century against Western colonial powers based on the Malabar coast of southwest India, in northern Sumatra, and in the southern Philippines Islands.[1] These activists were inspired by feelings of religious duty and personal heroism. They exalted the memory of slain warriors in poems and songs, thus inspiring others to imitate them. For a brief time, in very different conditions, suicide attacks were revived, among the Japanese kamikaze pilots in World War II, but the movement faded again after the war had ended, and in any case it is difficult now to determine to what extent these suicides were indeed "volunteers."

That someone might deliberately set out to murder others by killing himself is deeply shocking, which is why the names of these assassins and kamikaze pilots, notwithstanding their military ineffectuality, have become seared into the collective memory of every nation, and are now synonymous with either cold-blooded murder or world-renouncing heroics. But before the dawn of the modern age, the options available to any one individual bent on murdering another individual were limited to such weapons as daggers, swords, or bows and arrows. Then firearms appeared; Alfred Nobel invented dynamite, and contemporary newspapers wrote: "Dynamite: politicians don't like the sound of it."[2] This assessment was ironic in a macabre way: the "sound" of explosives was certainly audible in Russia when anti-czarists (who were already proud to be known as terrorists) used dynamite in their attacks on Czar Alexander III and his supporters. Explosives had become the weapon of the future for terrorist groups of all persuasions.

Cars were invented, and, soon after that, airplanes—and with flight came the ability to turn four passenger planes into weapons capable of murdering three thousand people, requiring only a readiness to sacrifice oneself, a limited knowledge of piloting, and a few box-cutters.

The ever-increasing rate of technological advances has made our world more vulnerable, and has powerfully enhanced the rewards of the suicidal will. All one need do is strap a couple of kilos of TNT around the waist, or grab the steering wheel from a bus driver, and dozens are dead; wield a couple of box-cutters, thousands lose their lives. And yet, despite this capability, the phenomenon seemed to have disappeared from global conflict in the decades after Japan's kamikaze attacks.

For the last twenty years, however, these attacks have become more widespread—as the profile of those who commit them has also expanded: Islamist and nationalist Palestinians attack Israelis; Chechen women crash trucks filled with explosives into Russian barracks; the remnants of Saddam Hussein's followers bomb U.S. soldiers, as well as themselves, to death. Moroccan Jews in Casablanca, French engineers in Karachi, American guest-workers in Riyadh, Australian tourists in Bali—all are targets for sudden strikes by Islamist groups.

Yet, while these attacks have become ubiquitous, real intelligence on who is committing them, and where, and why, is only gradually emerging from the shadows of false political assumptions and plain ignorance. Suicide attacks are a highly complex phenomenon. This book aims to piece together, in a logical sequence, what is known about its origins—which societies facilitate its development, what conditions are most favorable for its spread, and how the various tactics used have been developed. It undertakes, in a sense, a series of journeys: back to the early days of the Islamic warfare, and out into the specific locales of individual wars and peoples. For if one begins simply by lumping together all the groups that have resorted to using suicide attacks as a weapon during the last two decades, one is drawn invariably to the point where they intersect: the attacks themselves. If instead, however, the analysis is focused on such specifics as whether an isolated group or the majority of the population is behind an attack; whether the attack is initiated by nationals or foreigners; whether Islam or some other religion, or no religion at all, plays a role; whether the attackers are slum-dwellers or university students; and whether their opponents are hostile neighbors, openly declared enemies, or random

Westerners—then individual cases will be seen to be very different from each other.

Following the attacks of September 11, 2001, many journalists, politicians, and psychologists conjured up pictures of demons: suicide bombers were described as fanatics and lunatics. These fanatics believed, it was said, that they were bound for a Paradise, where they imagined there would be seventy-two virgins awaiting them. But even if this explanation were accurate, why would such "lunatics" turn up just now? Terrorists were already around in the 1960s and 1970s, but they didn't include their own death in their plans. When Peter-Jürgen Boock, a former member of West Germany's Red Army Faction, was asked whether German terrorists had studied suicide attacks in the South Yemen training camps in the 1970s, he said, no—"nobody who trained there wanted to commit suicide—and that includes the Palestinians. We wanted to achieve certain aims: we wanted to hijack airplanes, free prisoners, get money, take hostages. We all knew we could die doing it. But that wasn't our intention."[3]

Since September 11, a vast amount of information has been collected from many sources, and the last hours, days, and weeks of most of the attackers have been painstakingly reconstructed, down to the weight (to the nearest tenth of a gram) of the piece of soap found in the motel room where the leader of the attack, Muhammad Atta, spent his last night. But when it comes to the crucial question of how the plan could work—finding nineteen young men bent on taking along with them in death the greatest possible number of innocent people—these detail-happy reconstructions remain curiously opaque. The attackers weren't poor; they didn't come from the ghetto that is Gaza; they hadn't personally been mistreated by any Western power, far less robbed of their freedom. They were neither hermit-like fanatics, nor had they undergone years of brainwashing in isolated camps before being sent out as robots to steer the captured planes to their doom. On the contrary, the three attackers who had lived in Germany for years fell within the everyday spectrum of normality. Although they were at times introverted and antisocial, they could also be warmhearted and friendly. Muhammad Atta, believed to be the head

7

of the group, spent years studying at Hamburg-Harburg Technical University; his professor, Dittmar Machule, considered him to be a talented urban architect, giving him the equivalent of an "A" grade on his final dissertation, which took as its topic the preservation of a multi-faith neighborhood in the traditionally tolerant Syrian city of Aleppo. Atta would turn out to be the greatest enemy and destroyer in the history of another multi-faith, traditionally tolerant city—New York.

The attackers were strictly religious and, like Muhammad Atta, would scrape the frosting off the American muffins they ate, lest they contain pork fat.[4] They could live in the present: they enjoyed the occasional drink, danced, and flirted, like the Lebanese Ziad Jarrah, who, on the morning of September 11, called his girlfriend on the phone to say good-bye. They draped hand-towels over the innocuous pictures of semi-naked women that hung on the wall of a motel room in Florida, yet they watched (at the same motel) a pornographic movie on a pay-per-view channel on television.[5] These men simultaneously embodied two extremes, although, on the surface they didn't exhibit the kind of profile that would have made it even remotely possible to predict what they planned to do. And as for the appeal of the seventy-two virgins in Paradise—what use would Muhammad Atta have for them? This was a man so terrified of women that in his will he decreed that no woman would be allowed to visit his grave, that his corpse was to be prepared only by women wearing gloves, and that no one should touch his genitals. A man with such a pathological fear of women—aspiring to endless sex in Heaven? Unlikely.

Based largely on their experience with the therapeutic treatment of members of Western sects, psychologists have attempted to reconstruct the general methods used to recruit suicide bombers. They use terms such as "mental programming" and "destructive cults," implying highly sophisticated strategies of subtle brainwashing attacking the person's identity. "Sleep deprivation, withholding of food and drugs, surreptitious hypnosis, overwhelming the subject with sensory stimulation, and manipulation of feelings of guilt and fear are just some of the methods employed in order to destroy someone's self-esteem. The subject is given a new name and new clothes, and forced to carry out rituals that reinforce his new identity."[6] The same underlying motif is consistent: the attacker's soul is seen as a hard disk susceptible to being reprogrammed: "Here you have an adolescent from the slums. First, he's put in a Qur'anic school, then he spends months being prepared in a training camp. He's subjected to military drilling, ascetic exercises, and meditation. His brain is washed empty and then refilled with the truisms of the secret order. . . . His whole face assumes a smile of eternal bliss."[7]

While this sort of scenario would work well as a Hollywood film script, the real world is altogether different. Individual psychological models of interpretation, important though they are, can't function as the complete explanation. For while they do tell us something about motivations, they are completely incapable of explaining why these attacks begin at a particular time, and in a particular place; why they spread throughout the world in very specific patterns; and why some militant organizations have employed them while others haven't. Using a single model for all deeds of this kind obscures the fact that the paths that lead up to them, and the indoctrination of the attackers, are quite different in each case. The psychological patterns are familiar to us: in the same way that a sadistic concentration-camp commander could also be a connoisseur of the arts and a loving family man, the nineteen attackers, before they became mass murderers, were able to function as normal, unremarkable people. So what drove them to do it at all? What made them band together? John Horgan, the Irish expert on terrorism, warned people against coming up with over-hasty interpretations after September 11: "All we're seeing is the end-point, the drama," he said. "And that in turn dictates our assumptions about the nature of these people."[8] You can't consider the nineteen men of September 11 in isolation—but it would be equally wrong to treat all suicide bombers, from New York to Colombo, as being exactly the same. In order to understand the phenomenon, you have to dissect its constituent parts.

The clichéd model of brainwashing does actually work in some isolated sectarian groups, such as Ansar al-Islam in Kurdish northern Iraq.

But, it doesn't apply to the dozens of Palestinian attackers, whose biographies have been examined by the psychologist Ariel Merari; he has reached the conclusion that groups cannot "create" suicide bombers, but merely reinforce existing predispositions. The presupposition that the attackers consist solely of fanatical, single, uneducated men from the slums is simply wrong: women and secular people are just as likely to blow themselves up and, according to a study by Khalil Shikaki, a Palestinian expert in survey research, the readiness to commit such an act increases with the person's level of education. Neither is the unchanging misery of their living conditions the crucial factor; if it were, half the Somali population would have already blown itself up. However, what *is* crucial is the relationship between the individual and his status and expectations—or, more to the point, the thwarting of these expectations.

While the path taken by suicide attacks may have branched out in many different directions, it is hardly an arbitrary one. Why have Hamas, Hezbollah, the PLO, and other Palestinian guerrilla organizations, along with Muslim fighters in Bosnia and Kosovo, used these tactics—when the IRA in Ireland hasn't, nor have the Red Brigade in Italy, the Sendero Luminoso in Peru, Aum Shinrikyo in Japan? Why did this phenomenon begin in the Islamic world, and why has it moved beyond it—in some cases? Why have groups with no ties to Islam, such as the secular PKK in Turkey or the Tamil Tiger separatists (the majority of them Hindus), adopted murder by suicide as a weapon?

In the West, members of the Lebanese Hezbollah, Hamas, and cadres of the Algerian GIA are indiscriminately labeled "terrorists," but not all Islamist terrorist groups adopt suicide attacks as a weapon. Militants of the GIA, for example, set about slitting the throats of hundreds of inhabitants of one village in a single night, but never blew themselves up.[9] These groups can be distinguished from one another in many respects, notably in their use of suicide attacks. In some such groups, there is a fluid transition to conventional criminality and Mafia-like structures, whereas others put their "cause" above their lives and thus maneuver themselves and their followers into a position which allows for neither compromise nor capitulation.

The facile explanations for suicide attacks offered in the Western media lead only to further questions. If the attacks are to be attributed to radicalized Islam per se, why have they appeared only in the last twenty years? If poverty and misery are the decisive factors, how can we explain the fact that all the September 11th attackers came—so far as we know—from comfortably middle-class families? And if Muslim attackers blow themselves up in order to get their hands on the seventy-two virgins of Paradise, how can we account for such actions by non-believers, women, or anyone with sexual phobias? The obvious explanations are no better at accounting for the frequency of such attacks in specific circumstances.

Perhaps the thorniest question is how a society can come to tolerate, and indeed foster, a practice so opposed to the survival instinct as to be pathological. What are we to make of all those mothers and fathers who profess to be proud of their son or daughter for having blown him or herself to pieces in order to kill others? What makes an Iranian mother declare, in the heat of the Iran-Iraq War of the early 1980s, that she rejoices that her five sons died as martyrs, and only regrets that she doesn't have any more offspring to offer? And what would she say today, twenty years later?

Murder by suicide began its modern-day renaissance at the start of the 1980s, on the battlefields of the Iran-Iraq War, in which tens of thousands of Iranian youths, each with a little key to Paradise around his neck, charged towards Iraqi machine-gun positions in the name of God and the Ayatollah Khomeini. It was as if the charismatic leader of the Iranian revolution had picked up a silent antique instrument and made it sing again. By mobilizing the ancient sacrificial myths of Shi'ite Islam, a rebellious sect born 1,300 years ago in a revolt against the ruling caliphs, Khomeini successfully reawakened the notion of self-sacrifice as a weapon of war.

While it might seem absurd in retrospect, this notion, which cost countless thousands of lives without leading to any appreciable military

11

gains, turned out to be a successful export. Iranian Revolutionary Guards brought it to Lebanon to help their religious brothers, the Lebanese Shi'ites, construct Hezbollah, the "Party of God." Where the Iranians had prepared the ground for suicide attacks as a means of doing battle, Hezbollah cultivated it to perfection. Lebanon turned out to be a magnet for its most talented strategists and practitioners; in this tiny multi-ethnic state, amid intense competition between rival ideologies and sects, the Shi'ites of Hezbollah were the first to "brand" suicide attacks as "martyr operations." Following the first five spectacular Hezbollah suicide attacks in 1982 and 1983 in Lebanon, guerrilla-fighters around the world adopted this name, along with the modus operandi. All it takes is a few individuals ready to sacrifice themselves, one or more trucks, several tons of explosive, a little prudent preparation, and voilà, a tiny movement can take on the greatest military power the world has every known. The efficacy of those first Hezbollah attacks in Beirut and Tyre is not in doubt: they prompted the United States and France to withdraw their troops from Lebanon entirely, and compelled Israel to retreat to a strip of land in southern Lebanon, from which it subsequently withdrew in May 2001.

Suicide attackers are not cruise missiles on two legs, killing machines who come out of nowhere with the wrath of God or the murderous orders of a cult leader programmed into them. They are, whatever lengths they or we will go to forget it, people—individuals with families rooted in a given society. An individual who runs amok is capable of casting off all social attachments and allegiances—these cases can always be found in dictatorships and democracies alike. The suicide bomber, however, retains ties to his milieu and to the sponsoring group or movement. The very decision to volunteer for a bombing mission hinges on what relatives, friends, and local religious leaders have said about the actions of earlier volunteers. Suicide attackers will only be properly understood, insofar as any comprehensive understanding can be possible, by scrutinizing their spiritual-intellectual world, the ideologies that have molded them, and the myths they grew up with—even when these are as outrageously paranoid as the existence of a global Jewish-Western conspiracy against Islam, a theory that Osama bin Laden continues to promulgate to attract and exploit millions of adherents throughout the Islamic world.

The phenomenon of suicide bombers, as we shall see below, is not limited to those who do the actual deed itself. What makes the deed effective is its embeddedness within a network of reimagined and reawakened medieval myths and popular-culture hero-worship. This culture combines modern-day marketing techniques like trading-cards, film music, and video-clips, with a "creative" reinterpretation of theology that lends religious legitimacy to the attackers' suicides by characterizing them as the noblest form of fearlessness in the face of death. Another element essential to the success of this phenomenon is the preexistence of an enemy ripe for demonization. In the Lebanese case, Hezbollah was blessed with an enemy straight out of central casting— Israel, the seemingly omnipotent Jewish state already occupying Lebanese territory, in defiance of international law.

Hezbollah's successful creation of a modern-day mythology of self-chosen martyrdom led to its further export of this practice, which now vaulted across geographical and religious boundaries. By the late 1980s and early 1990s, suicide bombing had spread around the world in ways that could no longer be explained solely as shared religious motives or half-forgotten traditions. In 1987 it was embraced by the decidedly secular but intensely nationalist Tamil Tigers of Sri Lanka. It then erupted in 1993 in Israel, and then in Turkey, Kashmir, and Chechnya, until, most recently, thanks to the shadowy global network of al-Qaeda, it now finally permeates all national frontiers. Within each of these countries and regions, and increasingly across national borders, the effective staging of suicide bombings, and the dramatic political fallout they provoke, have encouraged widespread adoption of the practice by political groups of widely diverse hues. In addition to this tactical emulation, the bombings have also become a weapon of mass psychology. What German psychologists call the "Werther effect,"[10] in which the suicide becomes an idol whom others strive to emulate, has, in some cases, infected entire societies.

This can be seen in present-day Palestine, which, as we shall see, has developed a culture of death within its own civil society. Such epidemics are neither inevitable nor incurable, however, and approval levels for suicide attacks have been known to fluctuate dramatically in response to changes in the political climate. In earlier periods of relative peace and hope in Palestine, such as the early phases of the Oslo peace process, the practice was widely rejected. By contrast, in today's climate of daily Palestinian humiliation by the imposition of omnipresent Israeli roadblocks, with the sealing-off of towns and "preventive liquidation" of militant leaders—which can often result in civilian casualties, including small children and expectant mothers— the majority opinion is more likely to support such tactics. While this general acceptance of suicide bombers and the epidemic spread of their ideology is symptomatic of something hopeless and pathological, it may also be seen as a community-wide message of defiance directed at the oppressor: "See! It's not merely isolated individuals who are willing to sacrifice themselves to strike back at you—we're *all* ready."

As if to make a mockery of all Israeli defensive measures, Palestinian attackers persist in blowing themselves up in the same place in Jerusalem's city center—near the Sbarro Pizzeria, inside the Sbarro's, in front of the Sbarro's—as if to reinforce the message that no real protection or escape is possible. And the Israeli government's repeated promises to retaliate ever harder, using the full weight of its armed forces to put a stop to the terrorists once and for all, meet with the same response: still more attacks. Israeli Prime Minister Ariel Sharon, elected to office in the midst of a wave of suicide attacks, vowed to unleash maximum military power, to "let the army win," and to "destroy the infrastructure of terrorism." But during his three years in office, more Israeli civilians have been killed in suicide attacks than ever before. Every assassination of a militant leader of Hamas, Islamic

Jihad, or the Al-Aqsa Brigades increases rather than diminishes their destructive force.

The attackers, their supporters, and suppliers understand that their enemy is stronger in a conventional military sense. Yet they also believe that their opponent is weaker in a deeper, existential, or spiritual sense. "They have grown soft, the attacker believes; they want to live, and live well, and they are afraid of death." Despite their own obvious military inferiority, the suicide bombers and their allies draw consolation and strength from the assurance of this "cowardice" of the other side. They can only profit by it, of course, if they are willing to repudiate this "cowardice" and the reverence for life which they see as associated with it. This is the rationale for the (for us) irrational abandonment of the natural will to survive, and in its place, the embracing of one's death. When this fearlessness is added to the dynamics of a calculated struggle for power, the old rules of superiority, power, and deterrence simply fall away. Here is the Archimedean point by which we may understand suicide attacks.

It is difficult to imagine how the collective psychology supporting suicide attacks can be maintained indefinitely. By negating the essential value of life, murder by suicide has enormous psychic costs. No child is born with ten kilos of TNT strapped to its stomach. Everywhere—in every known human society—children are comforted, cared for, protected, and loved by their parents. Disabling this life-affirming reflex and instead raising children to an "age of martyrdom," in which they are encouraged (tacitly or otherwise) to volunteer to kill themselves and others, would tear any society apart over time.

We shake our heads in disbelief, or we may shudder, at televised images of ostensibly proud parents, smiling as they accept congratulations on their son's or daughter's martyrdom, and telling foreign reporters of their joy over their child's deed. But if these parents did not express pride, they would be guilty of a double betrayal: first, of the child, who would otherwise have died for nothing; and also of his faction, or even the community as a whole, which for its part is flattered that its struggle is now seen as so important and sanctified by the self-sacrifice it inspires. One can call it a kind of long-term loan, for which the terms of repayment are still undisclosed.

However technically simple they are to effect, suicide attacks require an essentially unyielding desire to walk away from what are sometimes relatively auspicious personal prospects. When suicide attacks take place in clearly delineated geographical areas, then society, too—or at least the attackers' social peers—are forced to respect what the attackers have done, and even to honor it. Any personal benefit from the deed must be in remembrance of those who did it. The belief in a future Paradise may well play a role in rationalizing the deed for many attackers, making it easier for them to go through with it. But if asked what sort of Paradise they envisage, those determined to die invariably give answers that are distinctly worldly: they want to be remembered posthumously as heroes, with their pictures on every wall, and they want to carry out God's will by hastening the liberation of their country.

Notwithstanding the pretense of traditional religion in which their actions are typically cloaked, suicide bombers are quintessentially modern, in that they have left behind the traditional interpretations of religion in order to exploit only selected aspects of religion. They are a mixture of the Battle of Karbala and cable television—old myths and new media. They have no ethnic ties to any particular culture, nor are they indissolubly linked to any one religion; rather, they are moderns, whom no God and no religious commandments can restrain any longer. To reach this point, though, they must overcome the single greatest obstacle that all monotheistic religions place in the path of suicide bombers: the ban on killing oneself. For in Judaism, Christianity, and Islam, the power over human life, including the right to take it away, belongs exclusively to God. But for the suicide attackers and their defenders—whether they consider God great (following Bin Laden) or dead (following Nietzsche)—it ultimately all boils down to a single issue: they take their lives and, therefore their deaths, into their own hands.

It is no coincidence that such would-be martyrs (who embrace death as they strike out at their enemies) appeared first of all within

Islam and, more specifically, among the Muslim minority of the embattled Shi'ites. Islam, in its political form, is a well-suited ideology for war. It first arose in the context of a political movement that included a strong military component, and the connection was never severed. The mental image of Muhammad and his crowd of followers setting off on a conquest under the Prophet's banner is easily conjured; a group of Buddhists doing something similar is hard to picture.

The Qur'anic term "jihad," like many other terms in teachings of the Prophet, can be read in a variety of ways. Childbirth is called "jihad," as is looking after a sick father; the exercise of willpower in resisting temptation—these are all jihads. At its core, the word means the "exertion" or "effort" of following "the path of God" for one's own salvation and for Islam. Obviously, there are many kinds of paths. A war is properly called a "jihad" when it is launched to defend oneself and one's community against the infidels (although this has never stopped any Muslim ruler from fighting his Muslim neighbors). The term has proven especially useful to Osama bin Laden, whose efforts to market himself as a persecuted defender of the true tradition have met with considerable political success.

With the growth of Bin Laden's al-Qaeda network, suicide attacks have detached themselves from specific local or regional problems and from pragmatic political programs and agendas. Al-Qaeda's rhetoric, at once deeply rooted in Islamic tradition and a twisted, aberrant, contemporary outgrowth of that same tradition, is able to unite followers from more than a dozen nations with nothing in common but a messianic ideology of destruction. The fact that al-Qaeda has nothing tangible to gain from its operations—it does not fight conventional wars in order to capture territory—is not a disadvantage. On the contrary, this makes it virtually unassailable. The network is everywhere and nowhere, using each and every regional conflict as a convenient staging-ground for its global mission. Al-Qaeda seeks out and colonizes existing conflicts, from Chechnya to Kurdistan, Kashmir, and Karachi—and makes them worse. It dispatches its own warriors to local scenes of conflict to recruit native volunteers, who are taught to see their heretofore parochial struggle against the backdrop

17

of a global war of civilizations. Al-Qaeda is an apocalyptic sect whose worldview has been successfully cobbled together out of disparate components, including conspiracy theories, the experience of genuine oppression in the homelands of its adherents, and the public humiliation of the Palestinian people, as broadcast daily on live television.

Over the last two decades, suicide attacks have become the most effective weapon of an array of terrorist organizations around the globe. However different their individual origins, programs, aims, and politics are from each other, militant groups such as Hamas, Hezbollah, and al-Qaeda are united in their exploitation of suicide attacks to hit their enemies where they are most vulnerable. Self-styled martyrs, from New York to Haifa and New Delhi, by highlighting the fact that their enemies value their own lives more highly than they themselves do, aim to turn the tables, and render the powerful powerless. Combating them effectively requires a global approach, and especially a grasp of the interconnectedness of such events, and of all these militant groups with each other. Groups from Morocco to Iraq are linked together as though by invisible paths and secret passageways. Thus, injustices perpetrated in Chechnya or on the West Bank can stir up hatred within Morocco and Saudi Arabia, and unintentionally provide aid and comfort to opportunists who stoke the flames of righteous anger elsewhere.

CHAPTER 1

The Original Assassins

A HISTORY OF FAITH AND POWER
IN THE ISLAMIC WORLD

You must not think that those who were slain in the cause
of Allah are dead. They are alive, and well provided for
by their Lord.
—Qur'an, surah 3, verse 169

Why are the Muslims backward whilst others are making
progress? Because they deviated from Islam—that's why the
Muslims are backward!
—Shakib Arslan, a leading Islamic modernist, 1930

The scene could not have been arranged more neatly. On the
evening of October 7, 2001—the same day on which the U.S. Air
Force started bombing Afghanistan—millions of viewers of the television
satellite channel Al-Jazeera saw a man sitting in front of a cave.
Osama bin Laden had gone public via video from his mountain hideaway
somewhere in Afghanistan. He was sitting on the ground
flanked by three loyal followers; their Kalashnikovs in view, they
drank tea before Bin Laden started speaking. The video was his reaction
to the aerial bombardment going on above them, and it worked
its peculiar magic surreptitiously but effectively. For the message that
the world's most wanted man so simply and starkly imparted to his
fellow Muslims worldwide was that nothing less than the rescue of

their faith from the attack of the infidels was at stake. Just like him, Muhammad, Prophet of Prophets, had fled from Mecca and its infidel merchants and potentates in 622 C.E., and, together with his closest companion, Abu Bakr, had found refuge in a cave after evading their henchmen by a hair's breadth. It was the moment of utmost danger for the prophet, who was being threatened by the forces of evil. But it was also a critical turning point: the beginning of a whole new era, and the moment when the calendar was restarted from zero.

Every devout Muslim who saw this video understood the intended allegory: the Americans were the "infidels" while he, Osama, following in the footsteps of the Prophet, would lead his people to freedom through a Great Exodus. All they had to do was join his battle and not betray the faith in the hour of utmost danger. Then he said, "When the will of the Sublime, the Almighty, sent a light into the world . . . , the most splendid of all the splendid ones inflicted devastating damage upon America. May God reward the power and strength of those who knew no fear, and may He let them enter into the highest paradise. . . . What happened in America is a natural response to their politics of idiocy and stupidity." In short: it wasn't us; it pleased God to train nineteen young men from four different states, to provide for them financially, and to let them get into airplanes, massacre the crew members, and finally fly into the Pentagon and Manhattan's Twin Towers.

Absurd!—or so says the impartial observer in this part of the world. Which doesn't alter the fact that in an online survey conducted by Al-Jazeera, only 8.7 percent of the 4,600 people questioned considered Bin Laden to be a terrorist. Most of them saw him as a mujahid, a freedom fighter in a holy war. Only a tiny minority of the Islamic world believed Osama bin Laden to be responsible for the attacks—even as the suspicion received the support of substantial evidence.

How is it possible to relate stories that are almost 1,400 years old, to rehash the earliest myths of Islam, and, by so doing, to achieve such shattering success in the world of today—or, more precisely, in the contemporary Islamic world? Whence this glorification of the past in the Islamic world, this view that a return to Shari'a, the Law of

Islam, and to a life governed by the revelation of the Qur'an, would lead to a resurgence of Islamic world power and, with it, a legitimate leadership?

Throughout history, Islam and power have been intimately linked. Islam—never a secret faith like early Christianity, which had to assert itself against hostile rulers—has always been a system of belief and practice and a doctrine of power rolled into one. Muhammad didn't do his converting in secret, unlike the Christians, who were persecuted for 300 years. In Christendom, two sources of authority gradually emerged: the state, and the church with its own laws. Islam, on the other hand, had only one authority right from the start: Muhammad, who neither suffered martyrdom like Christ, nor was forbidden like Moses to enter into the Promised Land. Muhammad led an army; had command over war and peace; levied taxes; created laws and bequeathed an entire canon of precise rules for behavior—for his era, at any rate. Within half a century troops had conquered an empire stretching from the Loire to beyond the Indus, from Poitiers to Samarkand, all in the name of the new faith.

With the rise of Islam, a new tradition was born, based on the notion that the primal event—namely divine revelation—was also the great constant, the eternally immutable. The future, by contrast, represented a threat inasmuch as it could bring unforeseen developments—in other words, change. A perpetual conflict thus arose between the authoritative tradition on the one hand and the necessity—though often unwelcome—of creative renewal on the other. This tension finds expression in the Bid'a concept of "forbidden renewal," a concept that has been used by conservative theologians throughout the ages who seek to demonize anything that might diminish their own power.

Since the Qur'an has, according to its orthodox interpreters, already "said everything," Muslims are expected to follow its rules. The very idea of "mutability" is tantamount to active opposition to the divine "plan"—a plan that, in the orthodox view, turns opposition into heresy. This view also allows the faith to be invoked and deployed in the pursuit of power.

Islam has by no means developed uniformly. Given its strong predilection for power, it took only a very short time for a group to take shape that embraced all those within the tradition who were *excluded* from power: the Shi'ites. In Iran, one encounters the odd phenomenon of Ashura, the public holiday during which the first three of the four Righteous Caliphs who led the Muslim community after Muhammad's death and who are revered in the Sunni world are cursed and vilified. In the eyes of devout Shi'ites, these caliphs were usurpers who had seized power unlawfully.

The split between the Shi'ites and Sunnis originated in a dispute about the prophet's successor. After Muhammad's death, Ali, his son-in-law, demanded the caliphate for himself on the grounds that only a member of the prophet's family was entitled to this position. However, Abu Bakr, a member of Muhammad's circle, took power instead—and Sunni Islam, called thus after the Sunna, the customs and traditions of the prophet, was born. The Shiat Ali, Ali's party, was defeated once and for all in 680 C.E. at the battle of Karbala—a circumstance that only served to increase the appeal of the embattled Shi'ite faith. The defeat at Karbala became a focal point for the oppressed and the subservient, and established a tradition that produced the assassins as well as the Islamic revolution of Imam Khomeini and the current, ongoing Islamic reformation.

In the materially prosperous and open-minded early period of the Abbasid dynasty[1] in Baghdad between the eighth and thirteenth centuries, Sunni "state Islam" developed critical and intellectual traditions, and an openness to traditions of other cultures, including a taste for the translation of numerous works of philosophy from ancient Greek.

Based in large part on the writings of Abu Ali Al-Hussain Ibn Abdallah Ibn Sina (aka Avicenna, 980–1037), and Abu al-Walid Ibn Ahmad Ibn Muhammad Ibn Rushd (aka Averroes, 1126–98), two Islamic thinkers, scientists, and philosophers who had developed strong followings in Europe, the school of the Mu'tazilites ("those who retreat") was founded. This gave theological discourse a new, rational direction. The Mu'tazilites called for the rational scrutiny of tradition, and valued actions led by reason more highly than the imperatives of religious dogma—something that stood in sharp contrast to the orthodox teaching of the unchangeable eternity of God's word. This was the era of openness, and the ideas of the Mu'tazilites remained in ascendancy for at least a century, until orthodoxy regained the upper hand.

The orthodox combination of faith and power proved more than a match for the Mu'tazilites' emphasis on reason, doubt, and disobedience. The Abbasid rulers returned to the practice of recruiting their followers from that branch of Islam in which obedience was encouraged and thought damned as unworthy of the faith. The Shari'a was drained of its entire potential for opposition—to the great advantage of the Abbasid regime. This tradition still has consequences today, connecting as it does blind obedience to a political leader with respect for religion.

Thus, the end of the Abbasid era witnessed a great watershed in Arab civilization. Islam's first seven centuries of increasing ascendancy were followed by a similarly long period of stagnation—in a spiritual rather than military sense. The Syrian essayist George Tarabishi, living in exile in Paris, sums it up thus: "This self-isolation of Islam heralded its age of decline, just as its openness during the period of its rise and initial greatness heralded its development as a civilization."[2]

The movement toward self-imposed isolation was helped along by the splintering, from the eleventh century on, of a once mighty centralized empire into regional principalities. With the weakening of the centralized power of the Abbasid caliphs in Baghdad, all manner of schisms and factions appeared on the margins. Among these factions, a radical sect arose in the second half of the eleventh century that deserves a place in history as the forebear of suicide bombing: the "assassins"—this, at any rate, is what they were later called by their opponents.

No school of faith could have been further removed from the ruling orthodox Sunni Islam of the caliphs than this little group of "faith rebels," calling for the overthrow of the ruling order—for their imam, so they believed, was the "true" descendant of the Prophet, theirs the true faith. They were an even more radical offshoot of the Shi'ites, who shared certain beliefs, but who were still awaiting the messianic return of the "departed" imam. As Bernard Lewis, the Princeton-based orientalist and biographer of the assassins, puts it, they were "a heresy within a heresy."[3]

During his long period as a traveling preacher and scholar, their founder, Hassan-i Sabbah, broke with the ruling clergy after calling into question their monopoly on how faith was interpreted, and eventually withdrew to the inaccessible Elburz mountains in today's northern Iran, a place no empire had ever properly conquered. Here he conquered the fortress of Alamut in 1090, never leaving it again until he was carried out after his death thirty-five years later. From here he unleashed his mission, using every possible means at his disposal.

What he spread was a cocktail of beliefs addressing many issues avoided by orthodox dogma: matters of earthly injustice, spiritual yearnings, philosophical questions concerning true knowledge, all embedded in a secret doctrine imparted only to the initiated—something that gave the sect its then more common name: *Batini*, the "esoteric interpreters."[4] Given the indissociable link between creed and power, faith and rule in Islam, Sabbah's repudiation of the idea that religious authorities had a monopoly on interpretation amounted to a declaration of war on the rulers themselves. These rulers quickly sent their troops into action in order to, in the words of Nizam al-Mulk, vizier of His Majesty the Sultan, "stem the pus of sedition."[5]

The "assassins," practically beyond the reach of the Sunni rulers in their impregnable mountain fortresses, could never hope to match in open battle the might of the ruling powers, so they resorted to subversion, espionage and, ultimately, targeted murder.

They conducted these operations in their own special way, as a contemporary source recorded:

Our Master . . . laid snares and traps so as to catch first of all such fine game as Nizam al-Mulk in the net of death and perdition, and by this act his fame and renown became great. With the jugglery of deceit and the trickery of untruth, with guileful preparations and specious obfuscations, he laid the foundations of the fida'is, and he said, "who of you will rid this state of the evil of Nizam al-Mulk Tusi?" A man called Bu

Tahir Arrani laid the hand of acceptance on his breast, and, following the path of error by which he hoped to attain the bliss of the world-to-come, on the night of Friday, the twelfth of Ramadan of the year 485 [October 16, 1092], in the district of Nihavand at the stage of Sahna, he came in the guise of a Sufi to the litter of Nizam al-Mulk, who was being borne from the audience-place to the tent of his women, and struck him with a knife, and by that blow he suffered martyrdom. Nizam al-Mulk was the first man whom the fida'is killed. Our Master, upon him what he deserves, said, "the killing of this devil is the beginning of bliss."[6]

This was the start of a 170-year-long series of targeted murders, which turned a tiny sect into the dreaded opponent of the great powers. In effect, Hassan-i Sabbah converted the impotence of determined men into a potent force and thus used a tiny minority to inflict fatal blows on the great powers. For at least as shocking as the success of the Fedayeen or "self-sacrificers"—as, incidentally, PLO fighters would also come to be known 900 years later—was their total indifference to their own deaths. They stabbed to death princes, generals, governors, two caliphs, even hostile theologians and Franconian crusader lords—but never attempted to flee. Instead, having carried out a murder, they allowed their target's bodyguards to stab them to death. It was regarded as a disgrace to survive the operation. They always used a dagger—never poison or bows and arrows, although these weapons would have given them the chance to escape. Escape was exactly what they avoided, for, in this cunning scheme of things, a man without fear of death was a man who was capable of anything.

The assassins saw themselves as the avant-garde in the struggle against the oppressors and betrayers of true Islam, offering the most extreme proof of their strength of faith by their willingness to die. Their opponents, by contrast, saw them as a band of deluded fanatics and murderers and painted the blackest possible picture of them. This picture made its way to Europe in the chronicles of Christian travelers, and ultimately gave them their name: "Assassin" is thought to derive from *hashshashin*, the "hashish users." The legend, much popularized by Marco Polo's travel writings, runs thus: when Hassan-i

Sabbah was living in his mountain stronghold of Alamut, he sparked the yearning for death in his young disciples with a cunning ruse. The men were given hashish—so much hashish that they fell into a stupor, whereupon Hassan-i Sabbah had them taken to a garden hidden in the grounds of the fortress. No sooner had they woken up than they found they were no longer wearing the same old rags as before, but robes made of silk interwoven with gold threads; they were lying on lush green grass and cushions; servants handed them elegant carafes of water and wine. The virgins of Paradise were there, ready to do their bidding, and there was more hashish, too. Completely off their heads, they eventually lapsed into a stupor once again, whereupon they were carted off and put back in their normal clothes. On waking up, presumably with a hangover, they asked their master what on earth had happened to them. Paradise, replied the self-appointed imam; or, more precisely, a foretaste of Paradise, a trial visit. Anyone who wanted to return there on a permanent basis would have to sacrifice himself as one of the Fedayeen, as an assassin eager to die.

That, in a nutshell, is Marco Polo's version of things, a version stitched together from the legends which circulated about the assassins in the centuries following their demise. This, of course, is the version of history propagated by their opponents, who accused them not only of indulging in hashish but of every other sin under the sun: wine, pork, human blood—not to mention incest.[7] There's a simple reason why the hashish legend proved so enduring: even then, European chroniclers were looking for plausible explanations for why the Fedayeen assassins were prepared to die. Much as the story about the seventy-two virgins in Paradise is trotted out to explain the motivation of Palestinian suicide bombers, so in those days it was said to be the befuddling effect of hashish, combined with a cunning trick.

The assassins' intention was to disrupt and destroy the Sunni ruling order. However, they had no realistic plan for what to do should the enemy be seriously weakened without actually being defeated. Once they had risen to the status of a regional power, they became increasingly embroiled in alliances and rivalries with their neighbors. Oscillating between the heady transports of messianic end-of-the-worldism and the cold and calculating business of killing people to order, the assassin sect lost much of its appeal and eventually met its doom in the maelstrom of the Mongolian campaigns of conquest. The sect disappeared without a trace, leaving behind it no tradition, no religious heritage. Its forts fell into ruin, attracting no pilgrims other than Western journalists, and travelers who enjoy giving themselves a quick dose of the shivers.

Although many writers have cited a whole string of parallels between Bin Laden and Sabbah since September 11—the retreat into almost impassable mountain territory; followers' readiness to sacrifice themselves; the ostensible terrorist struggle against the corrupt wielders of power in the Islamic world as well as elsewhere—there is in fact no tradition leading directly from Sabbah's assassins to the New York and Washington suicide bombers. The parallels are those not of origin but of aim; Bin Laden actually comes from the Sunni tradition, orthodox Islam in its strictest form, whose apologists attack not only Christians and Jews but also and especially Shi'ites, whom they vilify as unbelievers, heretics, and hypocrites.[8]

The real connection between Hassan-i Sabbah and Osama bin Laden is more complicated, taking a rather circuitous route—via Khomeini, the Islamic revolution in Iran, and the genesis of suicide attacks as such. Khomeini certainly drew on the common roots of the Shi'ite revolt against the rank injustices of the prevailing regime that also influenced Hassan-i Sabbah's ideology. And among the Sunnis, too, the readiness to become a suicide assassin spread from the Iranian war volunteers and the first "martyr operations" by a process of direct influence and imitation.

On the one hand, nothing remained of the assassin sect per se. On the other hand, something did survive of them after all—a kind of negative afterimage of their deeds, along with the popular fear of them and their readiness to die, which had just as disturbing an effect in their time as the suicide killings in New York, Tel Aviv, or Colombo do today. The very word "assassin" has come to denote the epitome

27

of murder, most notably murder through stealth and deceit. Thus it entered the languages of Europe and thereby acquired a permanent monopoly as the term for pre-planned murder.

The Mongols, who stormed the last of the assassins' strongholds in 1270, did not spare the sect's enemies. In 1258 Baghdad fell, and in the view of many historians, the Islamic world thereafter remained "outside history" for almost seven centuries. It is a striking fact of history, at any rate, that the Arabs, who had once adopted Greek philosophy and culture and developed it further before passing it on to Western Europe, lost contact with this culture and its subsequent development, and fell behind, by many measures of comparison, with the West. "In the Arab world, there never was this kind of break with the medieval state which used God to legitimize and disguise the arbitrary exercise of power," observes Fatima Mernissi, Morocco's most prominent sociologist.[9] Because no such break ever occurred, it still comes easily to Islamic spokesmen even in the twenty-first century to draw on their history, with its fund of knowledge accumulated over fourteen centuries, and in particular to use its sacred beginnings to justify their actions. Traditional Islamic teachings had retained their full validity; their status as the word of Allah had not been undermined by fundamental reform, by excesses, or by anything analogous to Europe's Enlightenment.

While the armies of the predominantly Islamic Ottoman Empire succeeded in the course of its 400-year history in conquering vast tracts of southeastern Europe, the cultural development of Islam still remained in a state of ossified orthodoxy despite—or perhaps precisely because of—such military success. Islam of this period experienced no equivalent of Europe's Renaissance, the Enlightenment, constitutional reforms, and transition to modernity. And after the devastating defeat of the Ottoman army at Vienna in 1683, the court and the military leadership of Constantinople were thrown into complete turmoil. As military inferiority combined with spiritual impoverishment, the Ottoman Empire shrank like snowdrifts in spring.

Then, in 1789, an even greater threat came sailing across the Mediterranean to the Egyptian coast. With the landing of Napoleon's troops—and of the scholars and technical experts included in his retinue—the Muslims finally came face to face with their inferiority in the techno-scientific age that had already dawned. Eventually, the French were driven out neither by the Egyptians nor by their nominal overlords, the Turks—but by the next invading power to arrive from Europe, under the command of the British admiral, Nelson. The trauma was now complete.

The attacking Europeans were no longer the hapless, starry-eyed crusaders setting out on mission impossible with cries of "Deus lo vult," with no aims beyond the conquest of Jerusalem (which they failed to attain). Muslims now faced an opponent who was militarily, economically, and technically far superior, and one that owed its great advances to factors other than its faith. "The Muslims understood perfectly well that the Europeans had overtaken them in power terms," writes the Tunisian historian Hisham Djait, "but it was beyond their comprehension that the cataclysmic expansion challenging their power was grounded in the fragmentation of Europe's entire religious foundations—this being the essential outcome of the Enlightenment."[10]

The battle against *external* forces further prevented Islam from *inner* renewal, and concealed a contradiction that developed gradually in Islamic societies in the era of European colonialism: Muslim leaders wanted to avail themselves of the achievements of the modern era without sharing—or seeking to acquire—the basis on which they rested. For the Islamic anticolonial movements had to shut themselves off from Europe and the West in order to be able to continue their battle. They could not radically challenge the basis on which their own culture rested, but instead had to positively rely on it, not least for reasons of self-belief. And thus the religious core of their societies remained intact—indeed, it became even stronger.

And it is here, in this dual reaction to Europe's invasion of the long-stagnant world of Islam, that we can detect the beginnings of the paradoxical situation of today, in which the radical Islamic movements readily embrace all the West's technical achievements while rejecting the political values of Western democracies—most notably, the separation of religion from political power. In 1930, Shakib Arslan, a leading Islamic modernist, posed the question: "Why are the Muslims so backward, while others enjoyed the benefits of progress?"—and, indeed, he made this the title of his major work. His answer was quite simple: "Because they deviated from Islam—that's why Muslims are backward!"[11] It was a question of finding a formula that would enable the Muslim countries to regain their power by adopting solely the technical and scientific achievements of Europe, an aspiration reminiscent of the—similarly futile—slogans of the East German communist project of "overtaking [the West] without catching up."

Just as the end of Islam's "Golden Age" is often tied to the Mongol onslaught on Baghdad in 1258, the demise of the idea of pan-Arabic nationalism also has a historically fixed date: 1967, when the Israelis smashed the unified armies of the neighboring Arab states in the Six-Day War provoked by Nasser. After only half a day, the Egyptian air force had been practically wiped out; and after barely a week, the Israelis had occupied the Golan Heights, the Gaza Strip, Sinai, and the West Bank of the Jordan River, including East Jerusalem. The defeat could scarcely have been more humiliating. The view soon became established in the Islamic world that the Israelis had won because they had adhered to their faith, whereas the Muslims had betrayed theirs and accordingly lost. In addition, there was the deep disappointment people felt vis-à-vis their new rulers, who had given their regimes all the emblems of a democratic state—they called themselves republics, held elections, and had parliaments—but whose rule was as despotic as that of the colonial rulers and, indeed, was often even more brutal. The combination of these two factors robbed the idea of a national state and the whole notion of adopting Western ideology of their lustre, and simultaneously fanned the flames of hatred of the West.

And when Muslims turned to their Book of Books for guidance in the wake of these events, what did it have to say? The Qur'an itself contains a heterogeneous mix of parable-like portrayals of Muhammad's life, legal speeches, prophecies, and exhortations covering every conceivable aspect of life. Those who take the Qur'an to be a sacrosanct text that must be followed to the very letter thereby shut their eyes to the fact that the "mother of all books" contains no theological or judicial system—6,000 verses give us only 200 clear rules for conduct—but merely the first building bricks for one. But today's radical Islamic fundamentalists, or Islamists, buttress their own power struggle by advocating a return to the Qur'an's message. This solution is of course accompanied by the belief that God and His revelations are on the side of the Islamists. The obvious problem with this approach is the fact that the Qur'an contains no system which would provide a solution to the detailed problems of modern society. Even today, the dictum of Ali Ibn Abi Talib, Muhammad's son-in-law and the fourth caliph, can be invoked against the proponents of Islamist orthodoxy: "The Qur'an is but ink and paper, and it does not speak for itself. Instead, it is human beings who give effect to it, according to their limited personal judgments and opinions."[12]

By tying the law to the revealed Word of God, modern Islamists deprive it of any possibility of adapting to a changing world. Viewed in this way, the Shari'a (Islamic law), according to Islamists, is understood as an unalterable code of law, subject to no historical change. However, as Islam expert and Professor of International Relations Bassam Tibi observes, "social change does happen, and the only possibility then available to us is to pay lip service to the law as it stands, while circumventing it in practice."[13] This divergence between the fixed ideals of Islamic law, and the constantly evolving demands for change that confront any legal system as its history develops, is one of the greatest problems that face Islamic courts when making their judicial pronouncements. And it is by no means a new problem: as early as the thirteenth century, before the Abbasid empire fell to the Mongol onslaught, social and economic life was already too complex to be based exclusively on seventh-century precedents. This problem was solved by a method characteristic of Arab-Islamic history. Islamic belief and basic law remained intact, but alongside it a whole new area of jurisprudence emerged: the Hiyal manuals of legal devices which demonstrate in both judicial and religious treatises how to circumvent common norms without violating the letter of Islamic law. If there is any bona fide tradition that today's Islamists remain utterly true to, it is this. Even the attempted justifications of suicide attacks must show some alleged conformity with Shari'a.

Islam as such is not the cause of terrorism and suicide attacks. Particular aspects of Islam do, however, lend themselves to being interpreted to justify a declaration of outright war against the West and against any opponents among their own peoples. They can equally be used to construct a democratic society. Both tendencies have been manifest in recent times, particularly (as we shall see), in Iran over the course of twenty years. The Shi'ite tradition of the cult of martyrdom and self-sacrifice, which started with the demise of Imam Ali and was revived by the assassins, burgeoned anew with the Islamic Revolution of 1979. And with it, a weapon re-emerged that had lain dormant for so long: suicide attacks.

CHAPTER 2

A Key to Paradise around Their Necks

IRAN'S SUICIDE BATTALIONS

✦

The more people die for our cause, the stronger we become.
—Ayatollah Khomeini

A space of time is fixed for every nation; when their hour is come,
not for one moment shall they hold it back,
nor can they go before it.
—Qur'an, surah 7, verse 32

Muhammad Salam is a relaxed man. A Lebanese journalist, he has
worked for news agencies in the Near East, and has spent more than
half of this time reporting on wars. He witnessed the outbreak of the
Lebanese civil war in 1975 and its end some sixteen years later. He
worked for Associated Press in Beirut, then, during the first Gulf War,
for some years in Iraq; he was summoned back to Beirut to take over
AP in place of Terry Anderson, who had been kidnapped by Hezbollah. For a long time now, his black hair has been streaked with greyish
white and twisted at the back of his head into a small cluster of unruly
curls. Muhammad Salam has spent a lot of time in air-raid shelters.
He has learnt to recognize grenades by their whistling sound, and
has forced bullet-proof vests over his massive frame. Over all the
years, he has tried to forget what has happened, to keep his soul intact amid the battles; he smokes too much, but other than that, his attempt has been largely successful. There's just one scenario, he says,

that still visits him today in his dreams, even though it is now 22 years since he witnessed it.

It was on the Iraq-Iran front at the start of 1984 near to the village of al-Usair, not far from the Tigris Bridge, where U.S. General Norman Schwarzkopf would halt his advance in the next Gulf War seventeen years later. After weeks of relative quiet, an Iranian attack had begun. Muhammad Salam, one of very few foreign journalists to be right at the front, spotted an Iraqi marksman sitting behind a heavy machine gun, his body so stably wedged in that he would be able to remain in position for a good while. His hand was on the trigger. And then, Salam says, they arrived. Or, rather, you could hear them first: a high, buzzing sound, as if a swarm of locusts were approaching. The sound swelled: thousands of human mouths coming closer and closer, all of them roaring: "Ya Karbala! Ya Hussein! Ya Khomeini!" as they came. As a human wave, they emerged from the trenches and dugouts, from behind ramparts and hillocks; thousands, tens of thousands of them, coming closer and closer. And almost all of them were children, youths, some of them holding Kalashnikovs with difficulty, others just with clenched fists. Every now and then, you could see an older man among them, egging them on.

The marksman with the machine gun started shooting. And he shot, and shot. And he simply didn't stop: "And he shot these children, in the same way you'd shoot at a row of empty bottles; he just mowed them down—and these were nothing but children. And they kept running; they were climbing over the dead, jumping over them, falling over them; and the man with the machine gun just kept shooting. What's more, from above, helicopters were bombing the Iranians, who were just running as if nothing could stop them." Muhammad Salam snaps off the filter from his next cigarette, and pushes it into a cigarette holder already blackened by tar. With a crackle, the glow at its end intensifies. "And at one point they really were so close to the marksman that he suddenly jumped up, grabbed his Kalashnikov, and ran off behind the line of defense next to us. Shortly after this, they rushed me away from there, when it looked as though they might lose this too. We had heard about it beforehand, but had never seen it with our own eyes: that's how an Iranian offensive works."

This, then, is how it works, the phenomenon known as "human wave attacks," the most effective weapon in the whole Iranian arsenal in the early years of the war. After they had been overrun within weeks of the Iraqi invasion on September 22, 1980 and had lost towns and whole swathes of various provinces, they went back on the offensive until the end of the year, won back the important city of Khorramshar in 1982, and were soon standing on Iraqi soil. But what a price they paid for it: every one of these "waves" consisted of tens of thousands of young Iranians, often as young as twelve or thirteen. They ran at the Iraqi positions until they either won the day or were all dead.

"In the case of another offensive further south, we reached the front the following day," recalls Muhammad Salam.

> A Yugoslavian colleague and I set off from Basra at sunrise. At around nine o'clock, we reached the area where the Iranians had tried to break through. There were bodies lying there. Just bodies—that was all you could see as far as the horizon. We started to count them. We counted them all day. We gave up when we'd got to 23,000 because we were supposed to leave the area before dark. We hadn't finished. And yet all we'd done from 9 a.m. until evening was walk up and down counting the bodies. The offensive was called Karbala IV or Karbala V, I don't ex-
> . actly recall which it was now.

This had, he said, been marshy terrain on the edge of the Shatt al-Arab, the shared and immensely elongated delta of the Euphrates and the Tigris. Corpses had lain everywhere: on firm ground, floating in the still waters of the bomb craters, and half-covered by mud, as if those following after them had trampled over their bodies as they ran. Many of them, their heads shaven, wore red headbands or scarves, and every one of them had a key around his neck—this, so they had been told, would open the gate to Paradise once they had died a martyr's death. "At the start of the war," says Salam, stubbing out his hastily smoked cigarette as if memories could also be reduced to ash, "the keys were still made of iron; they were the kind of outdated keys you'd find in bureaus or cupboards. But on that day at Basra, they were already made of plastic. Iron had probably become too expensive."

The "human wave attacks" represented the most disturbing and gruesome parade of mass self-sacrifice in living memory, comparable only to the battles at Flanders during the First World War, in which tens of thousands of men were hounded from their trenches into the firing range of the newly developed machine guns. In the seventy years since, no officers or army leaders had been willing to pay such an inconceivable price for such tiny territorial gains. The most striking thing about the Iranian "human wave attacks," however, was the degree of readiness to die. It caused Iraqi machine gunners to flee—not only because they ran out of ammunition, but also because they were driven almost mad; because they could no longer bear to shoot children the same age as their own. Until the 1979 revolution, these children had grown up just like children anywhere else: poor, perhaps, not entirely happy, but all the same, with a profound sense that it was better to be alive than dead. Now they were rushing to their deaths, as if the world had been turned upside down. And it was always the same word: Karbala. Karbala on their lips; Karbala on their flags.

Karbala: this name, which the thousands only too willing to die embrace as their personal salvation, is that of a town in Iraq. Close to it, a rebellious imam and his last seventy-two companions were slaughtered by the caliph's troops in 680 C.E. Nobody, though, could have had the faintest idea 1,300 years ago of the seismic effect that this skirmish, numerically insignificant compared with later wars, battles, and campaigns, would have. That this was why tens of thousands of children would run into the Iraqi firing line and into the minefields; why, only two years earlier, the Ayatollah Khomeini, despite being based in Paris, had been able to lead a nonviolent revolution in Iran that defeated a regime armed to the teeth; and why, twenty years later, Palestinian suicide assassins would adopt rituals from Iran that were essentially completely alien to them.

To understand Karbala and its significance, we need to recount a story that takes us back to Mecca in 632 C.E., to the Prophet Muhammad's death and the outbreak of the succession dispute: should succession be granted to the most suitable man from among the retinue of followers? Or should it necessarily be granted to a blood descendant? Two parties were formed; those in favor of a blood descendant triumphed at first, and installed Muhammad's nephew and son-in-law Ali as the fourth caliph. But he would be the last of the Prophet's relatives to hold this office. Soon the opponents of this succession got their way: with Muawiya, the fifth caliph, power shifted from Ali, and indeed from Mecca, into what is today Syrian Damascus. The second party, which would later enter into history as "Shi'ite," after "Shiat Ali," or "party of Ali," gathered itself around Ali's successors—the imams. Although they were inferior in numbers, they still represented a threat.

That, at any rate, was the situation until October 2, 680 or, according to the Islamic calendar, the second day of Muharram of the year 61. On this day, close to the river Euphrates and near the town of Karbala, the small squad of Hussein ibn Ali's loyal followers found itself facing the several-thousand-strong army of the hostile caliph Yazid. Hussein, the prophet's grandson and third Shi'ite imam, had responded to the pleas of the rebelling city of Kufa, whose inhabitants supported him in his battle for succession against the caliphs, whom they despised as tyrants and traitors to the prophet's message.

But nobody from Kufa came to the aid of Hussein and his small army. With drinking water running out, and the path to the Euphrates blocked by the enemy, Hussein, facing unavoidable doom, released his companions from their oath of fidelity and begged them to flee, to save their own lives. But seventy-two of them remained, saying they would rather die than leave him. Together they went into battle; none of them survived.

From the standpoint of conventional power politics, Karbala was a devastating defeat for the party that stood for the Prophet's succession through blood relatives. It was precisely the self-sacrifice and defeat of its followers that would allow the "Shia" to survive and flourish as a faith. In the Shi'ite Muslim tradition, allegiance is pledged not to the victors, but to the vanquished. Hussein and his followers made the ultimate sacrifice for the succession ordained by God, as they saw it, and for "the cause," the struggle against those in power in the distant West, seen to be illegitimate. Ultimately, according to the Shi'ites, the sacrifice was made for the guilt of all men. He, Hussein, had atoned for all who bear a burden of guilt. As Heinz Halm has argued, "Karbala is the turning point for the Shi'ites, the pivot of their faith; the climax of a divine plan of salvation promising rich rewards to all those who take up arms in the name of the martyred imam."[1]

After Hussein, who was survived by a younger son, Shi'ite genealogy lists a further nine imams. The twelfth, and last, according to the tradition, vanished, and has since then been hidden from the eyes of the believers. He, they say, continues to live at this remove until God allows him to reappear as the *Mahdi,* the returning Messiah. This temporary removal of the twelfth imam is said to be due to the threat the imams faced from their enemies (most of the previous eleven did not die natural deaths). So long as the danger persists, the Mahdi remains hidden. His return will take place shortly before the Day of Judgment, when his comrades-in-arms and his enemies will be resurrected with him, and he will lead his troops into an apocalyptic battle in which he will defeat the enemy. Then he will establish a legitimate rule.

This Shi'ite story of military downfall at Karbala has always held a certain attraction for those excluded from power. And when the Shi'ite faith became the state religion in Iran eight centuries after Karbala, it profoundly reshaped this country right down to the most detailed aspects of its faith, politics, mentality, festivals, and even the physical gestures and forms of greeting of its people. The high regard for sacrifice is still mirrored in the everyday turns of phrase and gestures. Anyone traveling through the blazing heat of an Iranian summer will repeatedly find himself being offered water; it is everywhere at hand in large, chilled containers—for didn't Hussein's troops suffer terribly from thirst? And people end letters not with "best wishes" but with *"qorban-e shoma"*—"your sacrifice." Flourishes like "I sacrifice myself for you" or "I'll die for you" are standard expressions of pity, gratitude, or straightforward love. The story of Karbala has been passed down over the centuries, and is told and retold to this day. Every year the battle is performed as a passion play on its anniversary, Ashura, when men run through the streets flagellating themselves. It's not always bloody, and not always serious. But Karbala is always present; it's at the very bedrock of the Shi'ite sensibility and consciousness.

Almost two decades after the Islamic revolution in Iran, when the country had once again radically changed, there would still be this empathy for those who sacrifice themselves—not in their own war any more, but in films as in politics. Iranians adore films like *Titanic* or *The Piano*—all those weepy films with their modern protagonists who are martyrs to private affairs of the heart, who devour one another, yet end up alone. And in politics, President Muhammad Khatami enjoys ever greater approval despite, or precisely because of, his being permanently humbled and impotent. We'll hear more about this later.

❧

It was Shi'ite fearlessness and veneration for martyrdom that brought down the regime of Shah Muhammad Reza Pahlavi, despite the fact that it was heavily armed and supported by all the Western powers. The revolution began at the start of 1978, after the Pahlavi regime's written attacks on Khomeini sparked a demonstration in Qom, the city of a famous theological seminary and Khomeini's main center of influence. The police appeared on the scene; they threatened the demonstrators and ordered them to go home. But the people didn't disperse—until the police opened fire. After forty days, in accordance with the Islamic mourning period, a memorial procession for the dead turned into the next protest march—during which, once again, civilians were cut down by police bullets. In a rhythmic forty-day cycle, ever larger groups of demonstrators coursed through the town to commemorate the dead; each time, more people were shot dead. Finally, the shah and his generals—or, at any rate, those who managed to escape in time—went into exile in mid-January 1979. A caretaker, replacement government installed by the shah at the last moment was swept away within weeks.

The Shi'ite spiritual leader who returned from exile revolutionized his country, as Lenin and Mao had previously revolutionized Russia and China. In this case, however, the leader was not in possession of a new ideology but claimed to take his country back to the beginnings of its traditions, its faith. Grand Ayatollah Ruhollah Mussavi Khomeini stepped onto the stage of Iranian politics to become the greatest exponent of the legend of Karbala.

On February 1, 1979, after days and weeks of uncertainty, an Air France passenger jet obtained permission to land with Khomeini, his staff, and more than 100 journalists on board. When they were still on the plane, one of his retinue pressed a copy of their draft constitution into the hands of one of the journalists "in case we get shot dead." The revolution was not yet over, nor was it clear who would seize power from among the loose alliance of middle-class, communist, and religious elements that were held together by little more than a shared opposition to the Shah. But when the Boeing 747 landed, it was as if the Mahdi, the hidden Messiah, had himself returned home. Millions were frenetically awaiting the arrival of a man who, despite seeing their massive presence, despite returning home in triumph after fifteen years in exile, didn't so much as smile.

The Islamic revolution took its course. With an incredulous world as its witness, a rigorous Shi'ite theocracy arose from the ruins of the Pahlavi monarchy that embraced the world of modern technology while shunning the democratic spirit of the modern age. The attraction of Shi'ite Islam was not the only reason—and perhaps not even the main reason—the Iranian people had taken to the streets and forced the Shah into exile. At issue was not simply a popular urge to compel women to wear veils and to ban electric guitars, although there was widespread discomfort with these Western, secular forms of expression. The Iranian revolution had been launched for freedom, for a more legitimate distribution of wealth, and for a democratic republic. Yet the people, including countless thousands who had once fled from the Shah's regime into exile and now flooded back, soon found themselves in a new kind of bondage.

Grand Ayatollah Khomeini brought into being a dictatorship of clerics. The 1979 constitution that laid out this new order represented a parallel universe unique in the history of the world, containing several small concessions to modern democracy while imposing a dictatorship supposedly mandated by God, which claimed the right "to pass judgment on the ideas, thoughts, and behavior of humans."[2] At the heart of the new regime was the *velayat-e faquih,* the "rule of the jurisprudent," who had to rule in the Messiah's place until his return. They ruled by the grace of God—and were not, therefore, answerable to the people. At their head was the *rahbar,* the leader—a post which had never previously existed.

Although the people were given the right to vote for a parliament and the president, the country's spiritual leader would rule for his lifetime and without restriction, over the armed forces and diverse paramilitary militias as well as over justice, television, and funds worth billions that had previously belonged to the Shah. Furthermore, he would also be in charge of the supervisory council that not only chose the candidates for parliament and for the office of president, but also could reject proposed laws. During his lifetime, Khomeini's word was taken as law.

This new form of government was indeed religious and revolutionary—but it certainly wasn't traditional. For the Shi'ite tradition does not naturally lend itself to revolutionary politics. The prototypical Shi'ite was the silently enduring martyr rather than the armed rebel. The attainment of legitimate power through the successor to the Prophet ordained by God did, indeed, remain the proclaimed aim— but it was reserved for the "hidden Imam" himself.[3]

A majority of Shi'ite clerics have always believed that the theologians should keep out of politics. The standard orthodox Shi'ite position is that it is a sin to meddle in secular spheres of interest before the return of the hidden twelfth Imam, the messianically awaited Mahdi. Until his return, one's task is to wait, pray, and hope. As one of Khomeini's early rivals, Ayatollah Seyed Kazem Sharietmadari remarked in 1978, "There's no doubt that the Mahdi will return, but he definitely won't return in a Boeing 747."

Khomeini was indeed regarded with suspicion by many of his traditional colleagues. He had in the course of the decades woven the trappings of faith into a political, indeed revolutionary program. "Islam is politics," he proclaimed, "or it's nothing at all." Whereas, for instance, orthodox Islam strictly forbids suicide, Khomeini was the first to offer a religious justification for self-sacrifice in the name of the Islamic cause. He downgraded the *taqiya*, the right to be freed from religious duties in times of crisis in order to avoid danger to life and limb, in favor of one's duty to the jihad,[4] and gave specific meaning and substance to all the self-sacrificial motifs in Shi'ite tradition that had become mere rituals over the centuries.

Khomeini reinvigorated and radicalized the faith, taking as his slogan the words that adorned many of the banners in anti-Shah demonstrations: "Every land is Karbala; every month is Muharram [the month of mourning]; every day is Ashura." Henceforth Karbala was no longer to be merely a passion story but the real thing, sudden and murderous, and Hussein's sacrifice, a model for every Shi'ite. The idle weeping for historical heroes would soon be replaced by tears for fallen members of one's own family. As for the clerics, they weren't dismissed, but, rather, took over power. The people wouldn't choose their leaders: God had already done the choosing—and had chosen him, Khomeini.

If Khomeini's return had begun the resurrection and radicalization of Shi'ite tradition, the war against Iraq, which broke out in 1980, offered the Grand Ayatollah a golden opportunity to further enshrine his regime onto the pantheon of myth. President Saddam Hussein's invasion of Iran on a 400-mile-wide front on September 22, 1980 gave Khomeini only very limited cause for concern and grief. He himself described the war as a "piece of good fortune" and a "gift from Heaven."[5]

Saddam had dispatched his invading troops under the mistaken assumption that he could turn the resulting turmoil to his advantage, and secure both a speedy military victory and the oil resources of the Iranian province of Chusistan. Instead, his invasion put an end to the deep political divisions within Iran and also fit perfectly with the pattern of history as understood by the Shia. Once again, the forces of the superior power were Sunni-sponsored—Iraq itself, and its sponsors in the Persian Gulf monarchies—and had attacked the keepers of the "true faith." The parallels with Karbala were uncanny, and Khomeini used these to his utmost advantage. The roles were clearly allocated, and every child in Iran knew what they were: if Khomeini had already denounced the Shah at the start of the 1960s as the "Yazid of our time,"[6] as the very incarnation of the hated caliph, it was now Saddam Hussein who took on the mantle of the caliph Yazid, and came to represent the powers of both the Sunnis and their Western backers. Khomeini thus became Imam Hussein, and the Iranian people were cast in the role of the proverbial seventy-two loyal followers, fully prepared to die. The war was an outlet for the masses whose self-esteem and traditional values had been called into question by the Shah's politics—undoubtedly one of the reasons for the conspicuously high morale of the Iranian troops.

It was during this war that the public in the West first became aware of a concept that would become firmly established: *jihad,* rendered in English henceforth as "Holy War." Although this was a military struggle between two Islamic states, Iranian propaganda branded first Iraq's leadership, then its soldiers, as "infidels," thus Iran was fighting a war of jihad.

The Iran-Iraq War, as led on the Iranian side by Khomeini, soon came to be seen by many as a war "by the will of God" for the liberation of Karbala, Mecca, and Jerusalem, which, in their eyes, lay in the hands of the infidels. Strictly speaking, an "offensive jihad" of this sort—one that is not solely for the purposes of self-defense—ought really only to be declared by the returned Imam. But from the perspective of Iranian war ideology, Khomeini was not just an ordinary though highly charismatic human being, but the Mahdi himself, the

43

Imam who had returned to lead the hordes of believers into the final battle and subsequently into the Golden Age.

In the first few weeks of the war, the invading Iraqi troops succeeded in advancing deep into Iranian terrain and capturing several centers, including the city of Khorramshar. The Iranian counter-offensive was launched in 1981. The Iranians moved slowly, lacking weapons, supplies, soldiers. The Pasdaran, the Revolutionary Guard, was only just being set up; the regular army was still weak from the purges carried out against officers loyal to the Shah. Only one item was in plentiful supply: people. And the Khomeini regime did what it could to persuade the people that the best thing that could possibly happen to them would be to die fighting the eternal Sunni enemy. "Can anyone who believes in the world beyond be afraid?" asked Khomeini, without the least doubt as to what constituted the right answer: "We must thank God if He confers on us the honor of dying in the Holy Battle. Let us thrust our way into the ranks of the martyrs in our hordes . . . if we have been afraid, this means that we don't believe in the world beyond."[7]

When, in 1982, they had regained all the territory previously lost to Iraq, the Iranian army command pleaded for an end to the war—but Khomeini insisted that it should continue. Thus the army, having only just gotten back on its feet, was yet again deprived of all its power, and in mid-1982 control of the war was put in the hands of the Pasdaran. No longer was the war about defending Iran; victory and conquest were now the aims. The new military strategy attempted to penetrate Iraqi lines of defense with frontal assaults consisting of wave upon wave of human soldiery without any kind of backup support. The strategy would finally be abandoned two years later, after more than 20,000 Iranians had lost their lives in a single offensive in February 1984.[8]

In order to find stocks of human cannon-fodder for the waves of attacks, recruiters trawled through the schools. They told the children the heroic epic of Karbala like a fairytale adventure, a grandiose stage on which they themselves were summoned to appear as heroes, as martyrs. A recruiter who could no longer bear it and who fled to Germany later went on record to describe in great detail how the recruitment process worked. On some days, he said, entire classes were taken directly to the barracks by Revolutionary Guards. The families were given only a short message that their son had volunteered to go to war:

If any children refused, we vilified them. We asked them if their parents perhaps weren't good Muslims, and wondered out loud whether we would have to send them to prison. Every evening, new children were standing in the barrack-yard: distraught, intimidated, and with no real idea of what lay ahead. There were panicking children; children who imagined they'd soon be with Muhammad, the Prophet, in Paradise— and children who wanted to feed their families by serving in the war. For every child at the front, the parents receive 6,000 tuman, the monthly wage of an Iranian worker. If the child dies, the family is given a "certificate of martyrdom." This means privileges when buying groceries, clothes, and fridges and, above all, high prestige and social advancement in class-conscious Iranian society, with its finely wrought systems of rank and status.

For ten hours every day, the children learnt to handle hand grenades and machine guns. Some children didn't survive even the first few days. They threw the hand grenades in the wrong direction or too late—and blew themselves up. After a couple of days, we had to test the youngsters for the first time. We drove dogs across the parade ground and shot them. The children had to catch the animals and slit their throats. Anyone who refused was given a rucksack full of stones and had to run with it on his back until he collapsed. After a week, all the children were ready to kill the dogs. Before the children went to the front, their parents were allowed to visit them twice. Any boy who cried when they said good-bye had to cart the rucksack full of stones around again. Slogans of Khomeini decorated the huge dormitories, and the Qur'an lay on the narrow bedside table. There were no family photos, no toys, no teddy bears, no mementos—nothing of their own. After their two-week training, the children had to function like machines: without fear, hope, feelings. We were forbidden to play with little ones. If we'd played with them, they'd have become children again, children who laughed and cried. And such children don't go to war, say our superiors.[9]

Among the children who heard the call to war were two fourteen-year-olds whose backgrounds could scarcely have been more different but whose enthusiasm was quite the same: Ahmed, the son of a poor tailor from Meshhed in eastern Iran, and Babak, son of a wealthy merchant from the exclusive northern district of Teheran. Both had listened enthusiastically to the men who had come to their schools and had told stories of how Hussein, the noble leader of the orthodox believers, had known no fear and had preferred to be massacred together with his last few friends by the infidel enemy than to surrender. If Hussein did this for all Shi'ites, then clearly he had done it for every one of them, too, for Ahmed and Babak, who were now to get the chance to be heroes and to be admired. Most children in Ahmed's and Babak's classes at school volunteered to join up.

But the lives of these two particular children were to take very different paths. Babak's father, wealthy and pragmatic, forbade his son to attend school for a while and bribed the mullahs responsible. Ahmed nagged his parents until they eventually let him go to the front. Loaded onto a truck, he was taken to an encampment—the last stop before eternity. The men then pressed a rifle into his hand and let him fire a couple of shots with it. It was already 1986, and the months of training children had undergone at the start of the war had dwindled to weeks—because of the death of so many trainers; because in the peculiar arithmetic of this war, it didn't add up to teach someone to shoot when he would in any case be shot dead pretty much straight away. The rest of Ahmed's training for his end as a martyr consisted in an amalgamation of religion and revolution, Qur'an and Khomeini.

After two weeks, Ahmed was completely sure of his cause. If he was so fortunate as to die as a martyr in the battle against the "infidel" Iraqis, against Saddam Hussein, the "satan" in presidential garb, he would make himself immortal. With his dying breath he would, clad in velvet and brocade, pass over to the green gardens of Paradise. They gave Ahmed a red scarf which identified him as *chat-shekan*, one of those who would break through the enemy lines. They hung the little "key to Paradise" around his neck, and on the back of his somewhat over-large shirt, you could read the slogan: "Imam Khomeini has given me special permission to enter Heaven." Thus they sent him into the firing line.

Thus, from 1981 onwards, they sent 10,000 children into the line of fire and across minefields. They were sent in order that their bodies would explode all the mines and thus clear the way for the soldiers that were following them and "because donkeys are too stubborn to do it," as a survivor later put on record; "we fought by throwing ourselves in front of the tanks, by leaping on the mines, by taking on the enemy with a stick or a rifle. We tried and tried, but we didn't become martyrs."

At the front there was sand, marsh, heat, malaria. Often there was hardly any water, and not enough weapons to go around or blood supplies for the wounded. But in all the accounts, the atmosphere there was described as being saturated with such piety, selflessness, prayers, and wishes to die that it already seemed no longer to be of this world. In the Iranian newspapers, daily reports appeared like this one by fourteen-year-old Ali Reza Najar Adabi: "We were eleven brothers when we suddenly found ourselves facing the Iraqi enemy. Then the Holy Ghost appeared in the sky and gave us new strength to fight. The enemy was soon repulsed."[10]

Many survivors say that those who died knew in advance that death awaited them; that they had dreams laden with significance the night before, telling them where and when it would happen. For it appeared to many that the death of a martyr isn't left to chance, but occurs when God wants to accept his gift. It isn't a matter of winning, but of dying on the right side. "Those who die as martyrs are totally convinced that nothing is more useful to the Mahdi's return, to his dawning empire as a whole, than their sacrificial deaths that clear the way for it. From the blood of the martyrs arises salvation, the tree of true Islam, not from the depths of the enemy. The importance of each and every earthly act lies in the world beyond: the triumph occurs at the end of time." Anyone who feels guilty because he is merely wounded may, in his capacity as a war invalid, bear the title of "living martyr."[11]

In autumn 1982, Khomeini issued "a whole string of instructions. In these, he declared that young people who wanted to go to the front did not need to have the consent of their parents. It was a religious duty to volunteer for service, and service with the forces took priority over all other forms of service."[12] In the same year, he rejected an Iraqi offer to send back the captured Iranian child soldiers within the framework of an exchange of prisoners. "War, war, until we win!" droned the loudspeakers over and over again; and the daily paper, *Etelat,* reported that progress had been made: "Earlier, you saw children there of their own free will, like mushrooms that had sprouted overnight. They crossed the minefields. Their eyes saw nothing; their ears heard nothing. And a few moments later you could see clouds of dust rising up. When the dust had settled again, you could see nothing more of them. Somewhere, a long way away in the landscape, there were scraps of burnt flesh and shards of bone lying all around." This state of things had, however, improved, the paper assured its readers. "Before they step onto the minefields," it said, "the children wrap themselves in blankets so their body parts don't fly in all directions after the mines are detonated. Then they can be brought behind the front and carried to their graves in one piece."[13] Any other government would keep such reports secret; but the Iranian government seemed to do its utmost to portray the deaths of the child soldiers as shockingly as possible.

The mobilization of the children was declared to be one of the state's prime objectives. Even Muhammad Khatami, acclaimed a decade and a half later as a reforming president, but at the time "cultural commissioner" at the military command center, was in the latter capacity one of those responsible for producing propaganda films in which actors on white horses, dressed as heavenly messengers, summon the children to come into Paradise.[14]

Many of the deaths were celebrated with a tradition that would find favor many years later with Sunni Palestinian suicide assassins in their encampments in Gaza: the macabre-seeming designation of death as a wedding celebration. Strictly speaking, it takes its inspiration from events of the Shi'ite tradition: Qasim, Hussein's nephew, fell at Karbala shortly before his wedding, and his wedding tent then became the repository of his dead body. It thus became the custom with unmarried men killed in the war to put a miniature version of the traditional Iranian wedding table with mirrors and candles in the display cabinets above their graves.

✾

And what of the families? They were divided in their grief. The brother of a man killed in action recalls how their mother "didn't cry, neither in front of me, nor in front of the others on the bus. But on the way to the place where they were holding his body, she sat behind me and sobbed the whole time, quietly; she didn't want anyone to notice. For we had to be proud. In the mortuary, she asked if she could give her dead son a blanket so he didn't get cold."

The mourning was in this case inherently ambivalent. People are supposed to mourn, but even mourning itself had to be sacrificed— for communal prayers and for official mourning ceremonies. The communal, public weeping for the dead, and above all for those killed in action, was, according to Khomeini, quite sufficient to gratify human needs. In a speech to the nation, the venerable imam said: "Weep, weep, if weeping brings you closer to God!"[15]

People were meant to weep, for weeping counted both as a prelude to martyrdom and, according to Khomeini, as a terrible weapon against oppression. He stressed that young people should on no account let themselves be dissuaded from weeping. For the kind of weeping or mourning that the rulers of the Islamic Republic had in mind wasn't private, not something that wrapped people up in their own thoughts; and it shouldn't have anything to do with the pain of saying good-bye to a loved one: it was something that should turn into anger and action; it should avenge Hussein.

The largest place cemetery in the whole country lies south of Teheran on the road to Qom: Behesht-e Zahra, which during the war grew even more quickly than Teheran's new suburbs. At its entrance was the Fountain of Blood, with its red-colored water shooting into the air and cascading down a succession of marble steps. "The Tree of Islam can only grow if it's constantly fed with the blood of martyrs," claimed Imam Khomeini.[16]

Years later, the cemetery administration has still failed to provide the exact number of graves. The files, they say, aren't there just at that moment; or the expert responsible for that particular area is ill; the whole thing, so the official will tell you, in any case requires official permission—and, with a look, he'll add: "Just don't ask. There are too many." By the mid-1980s there were already forty square kilometers of graves standing in dense rows, quickly weathered by the smog and by Teheran's harsh climate of piercingly cold winters and hot summers. Young people—twelve, fourteen, sixteen years old—watch you from the photos on the headstones; under the pictures are their names, ages, and then a place name: a village somewhere, or a battlefield.

Behesht-e Zahra is the place where grief was supposed to be transformed into an angry and bellicose desire to subjugate the enemy. Every Friday during the war, a vast mass of people congregated on this burial ground, turning it into what one foreign observer called the camp of the "Karbala option": "Within it there is a kind of second army, some two million strong. It is based on tens of thousands of mothers and wives, the same number of fathers and old people of one sort or another, and twice as many brothers and sisters and children. They are the families of the martyrs. They have paid their dues in advance, and willingly join the fanatics' camps. They aren't prepared to follow any logic other than that which demands the 'Karbala option.' They press forcefully in this direction. They are a considerable presence when any suitable opportunity arises, at every meeting."[17]

But as the war dragged on, the Iranian people became fatally disillusioned. The "martyr families," in particular, felt lost and betrayed. There were protests and appeals—some of which even reached the newspapers. These were the martyrs' parents, after all. This was their investment—an investment for God, but also in order to climb higher in class-conscious Iranian society. Yet the more wretched Iran's economic situation became, the more paltry the flow of state donations to the mostly lower-class families of the war dead. Worse still, it seemed that their sons and husbands had died pointless deaths, in a war that gained them nothing, for a society that was increasingly reluctant to be reminded of the war.

Ahmed and Babak, the two schoolboys who were fired up with enthusiasm about martyrdom, would both survive the war. But while Babak graduated from high school, went to college, and invested all his spare energies in organizing uninterrupted meetings with his girlfriend, Ahmed only gradually felt his way back into the world, one of two who survived from his group of twenty-five—stuck halfway to Paradise, blinded by a bullet after a few weeks at the front, far down in the south near Khorramshar. Once he was back at home in Meshhed, his family didn't appear altogether delighted. Now, Ahmed could no longer become a tailor, and his father didn't dare look his neighbors in the eye, as they had martyrs for sons—whereas he just had a cripple. While the Society for the War Wounded financed the school for the blind and Ahmed learnt to read Braille, Babak in Teheran didn't want to know any more about war and blood and martyrs and the whole obsession with death. Most Iranians felt the same. No cult based on the mass sacrifice of human lives could keep going forever.

The great ploy involving God simply didn't work out in the long run. There were just too many of them—too much "martyr inflation" (to invoke a phrase that made the rounds at the time). The price was too high, the result too devastating. When the war ended after eight years, with Iran's acceptance, on July 18, 1989, of UN resolution 598 and a cease-fire, its cost would be two ruined national economies and somewhere between 600,000 and one million deaths. And the prize? A border between the two states that hadn't budged an inch to the advantage of either side, never mind Karbala, or the "liberation" of Mecca and Jerusalem. An unfathomable readiness to become a sacrifice had led to an unimaginable, ultimately senseless, bloodbath.

However, the notion of martyrdom made a comeback in the aftermath of the Iran-Iraq War. We see it next not on a battlefield of tens of thousands of children, prepared to sacrifice themselves to gain a miserable few hundred meters of ground, but in the case of a mere four suicide bombers who sacrificed themselves to destroy a hundred times as many victims, to humiliate a superpower, to force its withdrawal from Lebanon—in other words, to achieve victory.

The Marketing Strategists of Martyrdom

HEZBOLLAH IN LEBANON

My husband isn't dead. He's now a martyr.
—Umm Muhammad, widow of a suicide assassin

The most powerful single force in the world today is
neither communism nor capitalism, neither the H-bomb nor
the guided missiles—it is man's eternal desire to be
free and independent.
—Senator John F. Kennedy, 1957

On the morning of Sunday October 23, 1983, a large yellow truck approached the U.S. Marines headquarters in southern Beirut. It was 6.20 A.M., ten minutes before the reveille which came, as it usually does on Sundays, half an hour later. More than 300 marine and navy personnel were still sleeping. Only the catering staff were up and about, preparing the breakfast. The sergeant on watch at the main gates saw the truck coming around the corner in front of the compound. He was unalarmed, as not only the airport's freight depot but also a large vegetable market were nearby. Then the driver suddenly stepped on the accelerator. He smashed through the fence, raced to the main entrance, and crashed into the building. With a violent bang, the truck exploded and, above it, so did the massive four-story reinforced-concrete building. Corporal Martucci, who had been asleep on the roof, was suddenly frightened out of his slumber: "There was a bang. We saw how the middle part of the roof simply rose up into the air and exploded. Then there was a kind of pause. Then the building, the floor we were lying on, collapsed in on itself within three or four seconds, and we fell down along with the roof." Most of the men were crushed in their beds when the building collapsed into a heap of cement and twisted steel. A few were lucky, and were hurled out of the breaking windows by the air pressure.[1] "I haven't seen carnage like that since Vietnam," remarked Major Bob Jordan with quiet fury.[2] A report in the FBI's forensic files would later say that this had been the most violent non-nuclear explosion since World War II.[3]

Colonel Timothy Geraghty, one of the commanding officers, had the good fortune to be already sitting in his office that morning, studying the daily file of press reports, when a number of window panes suddenly shattered. He ran outside and was immediately enveloped in a cloud of smoke: "I ran around the corner to the back of my building, and, again, it was like a heavy fog and debris was coming down. Then the fog cleared, and I turned around . . . the headquarters was gone."[4]

Only one survivor saw the face of the lethal driver. Lance Corporal Eddie DiFranco, who was on watch, saw the driver racing towards the main building. He was later unable to say whether the man was fat or thin, pale or dark-skinned; all that stuck in his mind was his smile: "he looked right at me [and] smiled. . . . As soon as I saw [the truck] over there, I knew what was going to happen."[5]

Twenty seconds after the bomb attack on the U.S. Marines base, a second bomb went off six miles away and collapsed the six-story quarters of the French parachutists who, as part of the multinational peacekeeping force, had also been sent out to Beirut. Here, too, the sentries were unable to stop the trucks speeding towards them. The whole building complex was blown sideways until it looked like a pack of concrete playing cards that had been toppled over. Fifty-eight soldiers died—the greatest loss of French soldiers since the end of the Algerian war twenty-two years before.

After a week spent working their way through tons of rubble— sometimes with their bare hands, or with tiny tools, in order not to injure any victims who might still be alive—the Marine rescue teams gave up all hope of finding those who remained missing. Like their kamikaze executioners, they had turned to dust. Ultimately, 241 American troops were lost.

Originally, the Shi'ites in southern Lebanon had welcomed the stationing of the Americans as part of the "multinational force," in the hope that the American military could put an end to the civil war that had been dragging on for eight years. But the Americans could only have maintained their popularity by adopting a neutral stance—and in the imbroglio of the Lebanese civil war, *nobody* remained neutral for long.

The catastrophe of October 1983 was triggered by the most minor of incidents. On August 28, Shi'ite youths putting up posters of Imam Mussa Sadr, the legendary Shi'ite leader who had disappeared five years previously, were shot at from a passing car. The youths claimed the shots had been fired by the Falange, a Christian militia, whose role models were the fascist gangs of Hitler and Mussolini. Once the accusations started flying, so did the bullets: fighters of the Falange and Amal, the moderate Shi'ite movement, started shooting at one another. The official American-trained Lebanese army, which had in the past managed to stay out of such gang warfare, was drawn into the fracas. The army won this battle in the end, but the Shi'ite troops were able to hold on to a large portion of southern Beirut, thereafter becoming increasingly aware of their power.

When fighting broke out between the Christians and the Druze in September 1983,[6] the beleaguered Lebanese army, hemmed in near the presidential palace in the Beirut suburb of Baabda, started to panic, and demanded the support of the Americans. In response, the U.S. military and Robert McFarlane, the special envoy to the Near East, persuaded Washington to increase the American military presence in the area tenfold. Soon an entire contingent of the Mediterranean fleet was transferred to the Lebanese coast. Thus the Americans took sides once and for all, and abandoned their status as neutral arbiters. Henceforth they became just one of the numerous factions in the civil war—to their great peril.

The extreme danger in which this policy change placed the Americans was sensed only by a few at the time, including Beirut-based Marine commander Colonel Timothy Geraghty. In reaction to the radio signal giving permission to open fire, he responded, "Sir, I can't do that. This will cost us our neutrality. Do you realize if you do that, we'll get slaughtered down here?"[7] His objections were ignored, and with a deafening noise, dozens of salvos rained down on Druze positions from the American fleet in the Mediterranean. Forty-three days later, Geraghty's fears were to become reality when the man with the smile blasted himself and 241 marines to death.

Who was behind it all? The Americans hadn't the faintest idea whom to blame for the attacks. To make matters worse, all the top intelligence officers in the CIA's Middle East station had perished in the ruins of the U.S. embassy in Beirut, which had also been blown up the previous April by a kamikaze driver.[8]

The smile on the face of the murderous truck driver noted by Eddie DiFranco was the source of the legend of *bassamat al-Farah*, the "smile of joy" that all suicide bombers allegedly have on their lips during the last moments of their mission. Smiling suicide bombers appear to be the exceptions to the rule, however. Past eyewitnesses who have survived such attacks and who have seen their perpetrators describe them as having serious facial expressions, "as if in a trance." Ariel Merari, who was later to research dozens of biographies of suicide assassins in an attempt to find patterns, similarly recalls no "smile of joy": "It's one of the standard myths—born of their helpless need to give an account of themselves—that the great majority of these men are cheerfully bent on killing themselves."[9]

Having crammed a truck with several tons of explosives, the masterminds of the Beirut marine compound bombing planned their attack meticulously, and took no chances. "Quite simply," as Colonel Geraghty said in an interview, "that went beyond the capability to offer any defense. When was the last time you heard of a bomb that size?" And he added, "There may have been a fanatic driving that truck, but I promise you there was a cold, hard, political, calculating mind behind the planning and execution of it."[10]

To this day, nobody knows who the deadly drivers were. A group calling itself "Islamic Jihad" rang up the news agencies in the wake of the blast—but who were they? Unlike the other camera-hungry civil war militias, they had no office, no spokesman, no face. There were no more than scanty pieces of circumstantial evidence and rumors— like the story that vehicles crammed with people had driven away from the Iranian embassy in Beirut only minutes after the attacks.[11]

According to American intelligence information leaked to Hala Jaber, Associated Press correspondent in Lebanon, two key figures were behind the attacks: Imad Mughniyeh, an explosives expert trained in Yasser Arafat's elite troop Force 17, and Mustafa Badredin, a member of the oldest militant Shi'ite splinter group in the region, Ad-Dawa. The attack had presumably been planned with support from Iranian instructors, in particular the Iranian ambassador to Lebanon, Ali Akbar Mohtashemi, along with various high-ranking Syrian officers.[12] Mughniyeh later rose to prominence as one of the world's most wanted international terrorists after organizing the abductions of several American hostages as well as that of the British envoy Terry Waite.[13]

Regardless of what group of radical Shi'ites was behind them, the perpetrators of the Beirut blast became world-famous at one fell swoop. Moreover, they had, in effect, forced the greatest superpower the world has ever known to its knees. This became apparent after the U.S. marines moved their entire force below ground and into ships' containers converted into bunkers, and especially after President Ronald Reagan announced the complete withdrawal of the marines from Lebanon the following February. The attacks on the American and French troops were, in the eyes of the radicals, glorious publicity for the spread of the Islamic Revolution—they had, after all, driven the Americans and French entirely out of the country and had forced the Israelis back into southern Lebanon (which the Israelis continued to occupy as a "security zone"). The readiness of Shi'ite assassins to sacrifice themselves without fear or hesitation for the "dispossessed of this world"[14] made an impression on people—and became valuable propaganda for radical Shi'ites in both Lebanon and Iran.

After the American and French withdrawal from Lebanon in February 1984, and the Israeli withdrawal of most of its forces in June 1985, Shi'ite militias ruled in western Beirut. They effectively displaced the PLO, which had been driven from the city by an Israeli incursion there two years earlier.

The Israeli invasion of Lebanon in June 1982 had been launched with the code-named "Operation Peace for Galilee" by then-defense minister Ariel Sharon who left his prime minister, Menachem Begin, in the dark as to the real aim of the operation. Beyond the limited goal of protecting the northern region of Israel's province of Galilee from future PLO attack, Sharon also wanted to deal the PLO itself a fatal blow. Sharon's assumption—shared by the Israeli army, and the majority of Israelis—was that getting rid of the PLO would solve the Palestinian problem entirely. At first, the plan seemed to work. Israeli units moved into Beirut, seized the city after weeks of fighting and shelling, and drove PLO chairman Yasser Arafat and his troops across the Mediterranean Sea into exile. But a largely unnoticed development threw a monkey wrench into the works. In the early 1980s, more than 1,000 Iranian Revolutionary Guards—the Pasdaran—arrived in Lebanon via Syria in order to erect a beachhead for the Islamic Revolution. Overnight, the Lebanese Shi'ites, the poorest and weakest faction of Lebanese society, had, in Iran, a powerful ally, which brought with it money, weapons, and men. Above all, the new ally came with a new, explosive idea.

Prior to the arrival of the Iranians, the Lebanese Shi'ites had been active combatants in Lebanon's civil war. Although the war had given rise to all kinds of atrocities—the massacre of civilians, torture, mutilations—all the factions shared the same primal urge to survive. Now, suddenly, influential parties were injected into the conflict to whom this seemingly basic imperative didn't apply. Brought to Lebanon by Revolutionary Guards, the tactic of suicide attacks began developing in the hothouse atmosphere of the radical Lebanese Shi'ite scene.

This is not to say that "irrationalism triumphed" in Lebanon, as German terrorism expert Rolf Tophoven has put it.[15] On the contrary, with the embrace of martyrdom a new, coldly rational form of cost-benefit analysis took hold in the conflict. That cost-benefit considerations can play a part even in a martyrdom strategy is something that the radical Lebanese Shi'ite group Hezbollah proved beyond doubt in the following decade and a half. Hezbollah officially appeared on the scene in 1985, but its cadres had clearly been working years before, as the group itself admitted by confessing belatedly to its participation in the first suicide assassination on November 11, 1982.[16]

In Iran, Khomeini was convinced that his country was only the start of an Islamic Revolution that was destined to remove Western influence from the entire *umma,* or Islamic community, and to lead it to a new era of political ascendancy.[17] While the authoritarian rulers in Saudi Arabia and Iraq did everything in their power to limit the extent of Iranian influence, in Lebanon, the conditions favored a much warmer welcome. Not only did the country have a sizable Shi'ite population, but no one was really in charge of the state as a whole. The weak Lebanese state allowed for a great deal of foreign interference, including the stationing of Syrian troops in the eastern part of the country. Syria's dictator, Hafiz al-Assad, true to the motto "the enemies of my enemies are my friends," made an alliance with the Iranian leadership in hostility to Iraq. Alongside his troops based in Lebanon, Iran's Revolutionary Guards, the Pasdaran, set up their camp.[18] Khomeini encouraged this alliance with his usual revolutionary *Realpolitik* despite the fact that in the very same year, 1982, Assad had crushed a Shia uprising in the Syrian town of Hama, killing thousands.

With the stationing of the Pasdaran in Lebanon, the forward guard of the Islamic Revolution and all its missionary fervor had arrived in the Arab world. But whereas Iran was a relatively homogeneous and strong state capable of defending itself against any kind of foreign intervention, Lebanon, a country half the size of New Jersey, was, and remains, a mishmash of faiths, ethnic groups (some seventeen in all), and social conditions. A single day's march can take you through multiple worlds, from the cosmopolitan culture of Beirut, to the inland communities of Armenians and Greek Orthodox monks, to the mountain retreats of the Maronites, a Catholic splinter group tied to Rome but whose priests marry. There are also abjectly impoverished Shi'ite communities behind the mountains, in the Bekaa plains; Christian enclaves further south; and, in the Shuf Mountains, the Druze—originally an offshoot of the Shi'ites, a people with secret doctrines open only to those who are born into the faith. The Lebanese landscape also includes Sunni craftsmen and tradesmen on the coast; and, finally, poor Shi'ite peasants in the inland to the south, who, in the course of the civil war, managed for the first time to become a real force within Lebanese politics.

Given the delicate equilibrium between Lebanon's seventeen different peoples, an Iranian-style Islamic Revolution was highly unlikely. Any attempt to initiate one nationwide would run afoul of neighboring factions the minute it started.

And this is precisely what happened to Hezbollah in the early stages. Taking their cue from their brother Shi'ites in the Iranian Revolutionary Guards, Hezbollah forced women to wear veils, banned card games and dominos in cafés, and attempted to censor dancing, music, and festivals of any kind, thus making themselves highly unpopular. The Islamic Revolution lost further appeal when the cosmopolitan inhabitants of Tyre were told that men and women were no longer to bathe together, and that they could no longer hold their beloved picnics on the beach. The dream of Hezbollah and their mentors of transforming Lebanon into an Islamic citadel with the aid of the Iranian Revolution, proved to be completely rash.

✸

Hezbollah, however, proved to be quick learners. Sheikh Sayyed Mohammed Hussein Fadlallah, the senior cleric in Lebanon and probably the most influential ayatollah outside Iran, put it thus: "We believe in exporting the revolution, but there is a difference between exporting the revolution as 'one unit' and exporting it as 'parts.' We believe that the nature of the actual circumstances necessitates its export as 'parts,' since only this will bring us actual results."[19] Early attempts to coerce the Shi'ite population of southern Lebanon to accept the *chador*, or veil, and other trappings of Shi'ite orthodoxy along Iranian lines were rapidly abandoned. Hezbollah grasped—as would the Palestinian Islamist group Hamas in the next decade—the political "market advantage" of combining dogma with flexibility.

Hezbollah also successfully positioned itself in Lebanon as a party with a difference. It refrained from the parochial spats of the old-line parties fighting in the Lebanese civil war, and shunned their pursuit of easy money. Rising above the fray, Hezbollah focused attention on the external enemy, an enemy seemingly sent directly from central casting: Israel and its army of occupation in southern Lebanon.

Religion, patriotism, and the willingness to sacrifice oneself can easily blend together when the challenge is to resist a foreign occupier of a different faith. In the Lebanese context of the 1980s, religion played an important role in the resistance, and the Islamist culture had created a psychological atmosphere of willingness to fight and sacrifice to the death. "Among Lebanese youngsters we can trace a permanent willingness to die for the sake of the greater social group. This is the consequence of the fact that the perception of the group in Southern Lebanon is rooted in the Islamist religion and the behavior of the group, which is based upon partnership and cooperation."[20]

When the Israelis first occupied the southern strip of Lebanon in 1978, a UN peacekeeping mission was dispatched whose very name made clear its intended temporary status: the United Nations Interim Force in Lebanon (UNIFIL). Stationed in the occupied south, its troops were supposed to monitor the "full and unconditional" withdrawal of the Israeli occupiers, as demanded by UN resolution 425. And it's still there, even after the Israelis withdrew entirely from Lebanese territory in the early summer of 2000, twenty-two years after their first incursion.

Normally there is a regular turnover of UNIFIL troops and officers. Only one man has been with the force continuously since 1971, and it wouldn't occur to anyone to replace him. Turkish-born Timur Göksel isn't just the UNIFIL spokesman; he is the walking archive of the history of this mission, as well as a subtle leader who, through careful negotiation, can manoeuvre deftly between hostile parties while remaining as neutral as possible. A massively built bald man with a gruff voice, Göksel has experienced the comings and goings of the warlord and knows them all. He has a Buddha-like calmness which can turn into a furious roar within seconds when the need arises—when, for instance, Hezbollah yet again uses a UN base as cover; when Israelis shoot at UN soldiers; or when, after the latter's retreat, local journalists mistake signposts for frontier markings and wrongly accuse the UN of ceding Lebanese territory to Israel.

Göksel, whose tiny office in the UNIFIL headquarters in the idyllic little port of Naqoura is brimming with paperwork, books, and kitschy emblems of all the foreign battalions that were stationed in southern Lebanon, can still recall the early period of the Israeli invasion: "When they rolled up, they were actually welcomed, because everyone in southern Lebanon was sick of having to carry the bag for the Palestinian attacks on Israel. But when the Israelis stayed for longer and longer, bombed Beirut, turned off half the city's water and electricity in the middle of August without even thinking about withdrawing—then people became skeptical."[21]

Maarakeh is a poor mountain village, where life revolves around two things: the Thursday market for vegetables, chickens, and cheese, and the mosque. In the late 1970s it had become a center of resistance against Palestinian guerrillas, and dozens died in bitter gun battles.[22] When the Israelis marched into Maarakeh in 1982, they were greeted by its inhabitants with rose water and rice. The Shi'ite community in Lebanon as a body had, in defiance of Khomeini's angry tirades, accepted the Jewish state up until then.

This state of things would last for a year before the liberators became the enemy, recalls Sheikh Ali Ibrahim, a local cleric: "For seven or eight months, there was no resistance against the Israelis because people thought they had come for peace. . . . But people here were deceived."[23] Serious opposition began after the Israelis founded an "Organization for the United South" in order to set up so-called village committees which, being paid for and armed by Israel, were supposed to create a kind of colonial administration.

The occupying military power adopted a carrot-and-stick approach to the locals: economic aid was promised to all the committees in exchange for cooperation. Anyone who refused to cooperate, and who happened to have relatives in Israeli prisons, was told that such refusal would be very bad news indeed for the prisoners. Uncooperative villages were also placed under the control of foreign militias. The Shi'ites of southern Lebanon began to fear they would soon share the fate of the Palestinians and be expelled from their own country. Their resistance to the Israeli occupiers then began in earnest.

The resistance began on a small scale, with the boycott of imported Israeli goods, demonstrations, and isolated shootings. However, it escalated definitively on October 16, 1983 at the annual Ashura procession in Nabatiye, when 50,000 people had gathered to attend the procession through the town's streets in which self-flagellators beat their brows and backs in remembrance of the martyrdom of Imam Hussein at Karbala. At the climax of the festival, the officer in charge of an Israeli military convoy insisted on driving the convoy through the crowd. He could hardly have made a bigger mistake. The myth of Hussein and Ashura concerns precisely the battle of those people who were prepared to sacrifice themselves against an over-powerful, tyrannical ruler—and the angry crowd, already worked up by the sound of lamentation and the sight of self-flagellation, set upon the intruders who were forcing their way through the narrow streets with blaring horns. The Israelis called for reinforcements and started shooting; and by the end of it all, several Lebanese were dead and fifteen more were wounded. The Shi'ite High Council in Lebanon issued a religious edict, a fatwa, exhorting the Shi'ites to resist the Israeli occupation—and the war was now official. Hezbollah had found its enemy.

"In 1984 I told an American journalist that the Israelis were making a big mistake," recalls Timur Göksel.

If they didn't make off pretty quickly, they'd soon see the flag of the Islamic Republic of Lebanon flying at their border. The Israelis were indignant, and asked who on earth this arrogant UN officer was. They still believed the Shi'ites were their friends. They said I was mad, and that it was Palestinians who were attacking. What Palestinians? I asked; they're finished! The Israelis quite simply didn't want to accept that they were being attacked by Shi'ites. They were, after all, allegedly their friends.[24]

Yitzhak Rabin, at that time Israeli defense minister, had initially praised the policy of "bombing South Lebanon until there's nobody left there"[25]; then, however, he recognized with almost clairvoyant speed what Israel's occupying troops were in for:

I believe that among the many surprises . . . that came out of the war in Lebanon, the most dangerous is that the war let the Shi'ites come out of the bottle. No one predicted it; I couldn't find it in any intelligence report. . . . Terror cannot be finished by one war. It's total nonsense; it was an illusion. If as a result of the war in Lebanon, we replace the PLO terrorism in southern Lebanon with Shi'ite terrorism, we have done the worst thing in our struggle against terrorism. In twenty years of PLO terrorism, no one PLO terrorist ever made himself into a live bomb. In my opinion, the Shi'ites have the potential for a kind of terrorism that we have not yet experienced.[26]

With the arrival of the Iranians, the radical Shi'ites in Lebanon had, for the first time in the civil war, received help on a massive scale from abroad: money, instructors, and the myth of an Islamic Revolution on the Shi'ite model were provided. But in order to do battle here, 625 miles west of Iran, a local motive was needed: an enemy akin to the Shah of Iran or the Iraqi aggressor. And Israel obligingly delivered it.

Hezbollah turned out to be creative innovators. Rather than imitate the indiscriminate and wasteful Iranian methods of the Iran-Iraq War, they turned suicide attacks into a precisely controlled, well directed and sparingly used weapon, deploying it to maximum possible effect. Local conditions, after all, did not allow for indiscriminate use of waves of suicide martyrs. Since manpower was in much shorter supply than in the Iran-Iraq War, human lives were accorded greater value. The total number of fighters mobilized by Hezbollah amounted to a tiny fraction of those 20,000 who were sent to their deaths in one single Iranian offensive.[27]

The radical Shi'ite strategists in Beirut and the Bekaa plains also needed to develop a rationale for the legitimation of this new form of terror. Under what circumstances could a human bomb be justified theologically? This was especially urgent in light of the fact that Sheikh Fadlallah, the highest religious authority in the region, initially refused to issue a fatwa to sanction the assassins, instead referring to the historically attested Islamic ban on suicide. The Hezbollah leaders finessed this by seeking out religious justification directly from Iran. According to Hezbollah functionary Ibrahim al-Amin, Grand Ayatollah Khomeini personally gave his blessing.[28] Sheikh Naim Qassem, the Hezbollah "number two," also developed, in various interviews and writings, a tortuously reasoned justification for suicide bombing. Qassem claimed that these attacks in fact had nothing to do with suicide. Instead, he asserted,

> Jihad is a fundamental basis for us. We do not use it as a means of imposing our views on others, but consider ourselves in a state of jihad to defend our rights. When a Muslim dies in a defensive jihad, he fulfils . . . his religious duty by waging a holy war as well as gratifying God by making the ultimate sacrifice. . . . Since we believe that our moment of death is recorded and determined by God, it follows that whether one hides in a shelter, is crossing the road or is fighting the enemy, he will die when his time arrives. Having established this it follows that when a fighter goes to fight a jihad we do not consider him to be taking any more risks than the next man nor do we think he is bringing his moment of death closer. So, all he has done is to choose the manner of method in which he will die, if he is doomed to die at all on that particular day. If you understand Islam, you will undoubtedly be able to comprehend that this person is not being killed prior to his time. From here we regard martyrdom as a Muslim's choice of the manner in which he seeks to die.[29]

In order to justify the attacks, then, a form of interpretive expediency bordering on presumptuousness was necessary: Hezbollah arrogated to itself God's role in determining an individual's hour of death. The decision to kill and be killed, as well as the exact timing of the suicide bomber's detonation, are very much in human hands.[30]

Little by little an entire culture of martyrdom arose among the radical Shi'ites of Lebanon. In the same way that the Inuit of northern Canada have different names for the various forms of ice and the Bedouins have an equally rich vocabulary for different types of sand, Hezbollah carefully cultivates a complex Arabic vocabulary for particular kinds of death. Since suicide bombing can't be sanctioned by Islam as suicide per se, the phrase *al-amalyiat al-istishhaadiya,* or martyr operations, has been created. At the center is the *shahid,* the martyr.[31] The figure of the suicide bomber is further referred to as the *shahid as-said,* the "happy martyr"; or, alternatively, as the *shahid al-muqattil,* the "*shahid* who died in battle," one who could have escaped with his life but preferred to die—like Hussein at Karbala. Then there is the more generic term *istishhaadi,* he who gives himself over to martyrdom— hence every suicide bomber. There is also the *shahid al-mazlum,* the one who didn't plan to or want to die but became a martyr to the cause nonetheless.[32] Hezbollah leaders developed this latter term to describe those sitting in the passenger seats of exploding vehicles that had been packed with tons of TNT. (Israeli military commanders in Lebanon had ordered that a minimum of two people occupy every moving car in the occupied zone, on the assumption that the suicide bombers, whom they considered fanatics running amok, would only act alone, and that this edict would thus stamp out suicide car bombings.[33] Henceforth, Hezbollah's death announcements praised the driver of an exploded car as a *shahid as-said,* a "happy martyr"; the passenger, a *shahid al-mazlum* ("unintentional martyr"), received, so to speak, a second-class ticket to Paradise.

A cult, then, was established around the martyrs. In Hezbollah newspapers, on their radio broadcasts, and, since the 1990s, on their own television station, the martyrs' names and deeds are praised. Their farewell videos, recorded before the attack, are broadcast, as are pictures of the attack itself. The preachers in the mosques hold them up as examples. Widows of dead bombers are also given an official title: *awalat ash-shuhada,* or "martyr widows."[34] A "martyrs' fund" takes care of the widow's maintenance, and a network of day-care centers looks after the children left behind. (It seems paradoxical that the groups offering the most comprehensive social welfare services are also the most ardent proponents of suicide bombing, but this social safety net allows the strategy of intentional martyrdom to maintain popular support.)

After its first devastating attacks on American, French, and Israeli targets, Hezbollah leaders throughout the 1980s focused their bombs-on-wheels on Israeli military convoys, artillery positions, and barracks in southern Lebanon. The delivery method varied widely; they used cars loaded with 150–900 kg of explosive, explosive-laden belts (which later were widely adopted by suicide bombers in Israel proper and in Sri Lanka), and, in a few cases, donkeys and boats. The number of organizations serving as instigators expanded as well. Even as Hezbollah itself reduced the frequency of its attacks in the course of the 1980s, copycat groups of all sorts now came out of the woodwork. Less than half of the fifty or so suicide attacks from 1983 onwards were credited to Hezbollah; the rest were committed by Amal or the secular groups controlled by Syria—whom nobody remembers any more.

The suicide attacks decreased dramatically in the course of the 1990s in Lebanon, however, constituting less than one-half of one percent of Hezbollah military activity during this period. In 1999, the Israeli army counted 1,500 Hezbollah-instigated military operations during the 1990s, only one of which was a suicide bombing. The reasons for this dramatic drop-off are many and varied. Improved security for buildings and convoys have made it harder to kill a lot of people in one fell swoop. Moreover, Hezbollah itself, being a small organization with a serious manpower shortage, can scarcely afford to encourage all of its fighters to avail themselves of this ultimate weapon. They have developed other weapons of choice: sophisticated bombs detonated by remote control; reconnaissance; espionage; special forces units; and abductions of Israeli soldiers. Perhaps most important, Hezbollah drew back from suicide bombing because of its own success: from an initial position of inferiority, Hezbollah had become a powerful regional force. A nimble, highly flexible organization that has steered its way through the storms of Lebanese politics with astounding adroitness, it no longer needs to demand the ultimate form of self-sacrifice from its followers.

Israel's leadership in fact unintentionally contributed to the rise in stature of Hezbollah when, on February 16, 1992, missiles fired by Israeli helicopter gunships incinerated the Hezbollah founder and Secretary-General Sheikh Abbas al-Mussawi, along with his wife, their one-year-old child, and several bodyguards on a road southeast of the town of Sidon.[35] Tens of thousands of Lebanese came to the funeral the following day, giving the organization a mighty boost during a period in which the majority of Lebanese were fed up with the fighting and were longing for peace.

Their country practically destroyed and their economy in tatters, the Lebanese might well have turned their backs on the idea of an Islamic state. But this assassination, combined with the April 1996 Israeli army's "Operation Grapes of Wrath" offensive, with its bombardment of Hezbollah bases in southern Lebanon and Beirut power stations, at the cost of 200 Lebanese lives, pushed many Lebanese of all faiths, Muslims and Christians alike, into the arms of Hezbollah.

It is more difficult to make direct contact with Hezbollah than with other political groups. Its press office is located in Haret ar-Rek, an overpopulated district of southern Beirut, somewhere within the nooks and crannies of a sprawling mass of never-quite-finished houses, illegal add-ons, and streets that are far too narrow, made even narrower by the carts of traveling traders. Shop counters in this neighborhood display the signature Hezbollah donation tins shaped in the form of Jerusalem's Dome of the Rock. Banners over the street with the "Party of God" logo in the calligraphic form of a Kalashnikov clearly show who's in control in these overpopulated slums. On this autumn day in October 1997 I have been given only vague directions to the press office, which is supposed to be on the third floor of a nondescript concrete building on a side street, but I see no sign outside and no name beside the bell. In the end, however, I don't have to find Hezbollah: Hezbollah finds me.

I am approached on the street by a young man who politely asks what I'm after. I want to speak to someone from Hezbollah, I reply. The man gives me a curt nod, and beckons me to follow him through seething crowds and through a house entrance, opposite a candy store.

Inside, in a conference room filled with brown corduroy armchairs, a self-produced video clip runs in an endless loop. "Two sides of the same terrorism," the title announces and, to the accompaniment of dramatic music, a blazing tablet with the Star of David on one side and the Stars and Stripes on the other appears. Hezbollah spokesman Ibrahim Mussawi is in rather a bad mood as he sits in his office next door. "Of course we want Israel to withdraw from southern Lebanon but obviously, we will keep our options open on whether we'll stop the war or not."

Mussawi's reluctance to talk peace is understandable. Although Hezbollah maintains schools and hospitals and runs social welfare facilities across half the country, the core of its political identity is still the battle in the occupied south. Mussawi makes it clear to me how important it is for his group to maintain—and use—the memory of martyrs who have fallen in the cause. He speaks with reverence of the mothers' and wives' willingness to make sacrifices, performing his PR duties in an irritatingly cloying manner. "Do you want to meet the widow of a martyr?" That wouldn't be a problem. But it would be appreciated if I refrained from offering any condolences: "Our *awalat ash-shuhada* [martyr widows] are proud of their fate."

The next day, we sit with Maha Talib, the widow of the "esteemed martyr" Saleh Gandour. The father of three children, he rammed his

68

car loaded with 450 kg of explosives into an Israeli convoy on May 25, 1995—an event recorded for posterity by a Hezbollah camera crew. The video footage appeared on the following evening's news on almost all Lebanese television stations. At a press conference after Saleh Gandour's attack, a Hezbollah spokesman claimed that the leadership had agonized over whether to send the father of three children on a suicide mission. In the end, he said, they decided that to do otherwise would have dissuaded many potential male martyrs from obeying another command of their faith: to marry and have a family.

Twenty-five-year-old Maha Talib, a petite woman, maintains her apartment as a shrine to her deceased husband. Several walls are papered with photos of Saleh with local politicians, Saleh with a Kalashnikov, Saleh with the Qur'an. Never Saleh with her. It had been clear to her right from the start, when they met in 1989 in a Beirut slum, that he was looking forward not to a long life together with her, but to his dream of death by martyrdom. Even before their marriage, Saleh was an active member of the "Islamic Resistance," as she puts it. He repeatedly disappeared to prepare attacks and his own "martyr operation" in the south. Maha knew what he was doing and accepted it,

> but two weeks before it happened, I became frightened that I'd never see him again. When I asked him, he said yes, I was right. I begged him not to leave us, but there was nothing for it. What would become of our daughter who was only four months old? But he just replied, "You've always known this is what I was destined to do." Even if I'd tried to stop him, it wouldn't have worked. This was his path; he'd dreamed of it for so long; for three years he'd pleaded with the leadership to send him on a mission, until they eventually let him have his wish—even though they don't normally let fathers go. At the end of the day, he had one single aim: to kill as many of his enemies as possible. He believed that he had to defend his country, and that this was the best way to do so.

Maha Talib speaks in a practiced manner, looking almost cheerful. "My husband's death has made me proud and happy," she repeats three times, like a mantra. The jihad, she says, is an honor, a duty. It sounds as if this phrase has already been said once too often, and no longer expresses what is really going on inside a woman who has three small children by a man who took his leave of them in order to blow up himself and others; but this is her story, and Hezbollah couldn't have wished for a better narrator.

Maha Talib senses my distress and disbelief. She looks me in the eye and says softly, "Of course, it's always sad when people lose the ones they love the most. But my husband died for his country. He did it for all of us, and showed Israel that its soldiers won't have a quiet second so long as they occupy our country! I really don't feel that I've entirely lost him. I dream about him almost every night." Then her five-year-old son Muhammad comes trotting through the room to the family's video machine, and presses the start button. The video begins with a shot of a single tree, followed by a row of houses, then a pale landscape, all of it a bit shaky. Then there's an orangey-red fireball, and the little boy points to the TV screen saying "Papa!" Muhammad is delighted; Maha Talib smiles and says, looking at him, "If he should decide to follow his father one day, I wouldn't stand in his way."

There seems to be no space for grief, as the widow and her family are charged with a weighty task: to be living proof of the fact that Saleh Gandour's mission, which cost the lives of twelve Israeli soldiers in addition to his own, wasn't the deed of a desperate individual. Hezbollah wants to persuade the world that Gandour's suicide bombing mission was just as much a part of the life of a Shi'ite resistance fighter as getting married, bringing up children, leading a normal everyday life. Hezbollah undertakes to pay all education and living expenses of the surviving immediate family. On occasion it even succeeds in overruling the wishes of tradition-conscious fathers-in-law who demand that their son's widow and her children take up residence in their households; if the widow wants to live alone with her children, Hezbollah makes sure she can do so.

The following day, I am on the road south of Beirut, heading twenty-seven miles south to the Shi'ite town of Nabatiye. This is the front, where Hezbollah and the Israeli military, positioned on the hilltops above the town, stare each other down. Sounds of war are all around. Nabatiye is a stronghold of the "Party of God," and a town renowned for its annual Ashura festival.

Death is at home here, and Ahmed Saad, video-cameraman and local Hezbollah functionary, makes his living out of it. "Wedding videos on the right; martyr videos on the left," is how he describes his archive. Martyr videos? "You know, featuring bodies laid out; lamentations; processions through the town; burials; gun salutes; all professionally edited." A lucrative way to make a living in this day and age. After showing off his archive, Saad goes into raptures about French film star Catherine Deneuve, then takes me to see yet another widow of a martyr, Umm Muhammad. She is a charming, well-educated young woman. Unfortunately, our interview is hampered by the deafening explosions of the Lebanese anti-aircraft guns, firing at two Israeli jets that have just bombed a Hezbollah position. I am also unnerved by her insistence on speaking of her husband, who died months before as an official Hezbollah martyr, in the present tense: "My husband is a martyr. Very well then, he is now in paradise. It was sad for him to be already over thirty and still not a martyr. He was miserable on his birthday. I said to him then: don't worry, you'll get your wish. For us, it's normal to live like that."

She has to break off at this point to go to her English course in the American Language Center: "You've got to make something of yourself!" Education is, she says, terribly important, and death in itself isn't a tragic event. There is a life before death and one afterwards: it's as simple as that. She is the beneficiary of a Hezbollah martyr fund known as the Khomeini Aid Program, which pays for the schooling of her children and the upkeep of her family. Her husband was an office worker by day and a fighter by night—just like many others of the hard core of the 300 to 400 professional guerrillas who pursue normal day jobs as bakers, teachers, shopkeepers, and whose neighbors often don't know what they do the rest of the time.

The very evening of the day she first received the news of her husband's death, Umm Muhammad gave birth to Muhammad Ali, her fourth child and first son. Unprompted, she comes out with the same line as Maha Talib in the course of our discussion: "If my son decides to go the same way, I'll help him to do it." For now, though, he's just learning to walk. "My husband is fine. I miss him. But please excuse me; I really do have to go now."

Can this be genuine, I wonder? How can anyone who has lost a son, a husband, a father, feel delight and satisfaction, rather than grief and pain? Surely this expression of joy is an act? "Not necessarily," says a Lebanese journalist colleague who has spoken to dozens of the bereaved, and who has always encountered the same reaction. "It's both at the same time: they cry and they're proud. They're proud of his death and of their grief. It seems to work. And journalists never get to see the people who go to pieces. Hezbollah always gets there first."

In the south of the country Hezbollah has become a state within the state, or, to put it more precisely, it operates *instead* of the state, because in Lebanon the government has no presence in areas where citizens have need of public services. The organization's two faces—its military wing, with its careful endorsement of (despite decreasing enthusiasm for) suicide bombing tactics, and its social welfare wing—appear to come together on a doctors' bulletin board in a new Hezbollah hospital, where pictures of dead local martyrs are pinned up next to the laboratory's blood reference tables.

Hezbollah pays for three mobile clinics for southern Lebanese villages as well as for the local office of the Khomeini Aid Program and the best school in the area, Madrasa al-Mahdi, which features time clocks for the teachers and two months' compulsory teacher enrichment training every year, in cooperation with the French cultural center. The curriculum is recognized by the Lebanese Ministry for Education—not that official recognition from a practically nonexistent state agency means much. The sound of French lessons spills out of classrooms into the corridor. "Nothing beats a good education," says the energetic headmistress from under her headscarf. Her four-year-old pupils start to learn languages by singing songs, and begin reading them at six. Of course, they are taught the Qur'an. "We try to be as modern as possible, pedagogically speaking," she continues, acknowledging that the school couldn't have been built without Iranian money. The school has an auditorium featuring a stage with painted-on Smurf backdrops and other decorations, a stereo system, and loudspeakers. It also has a canteen advertising Pepsi, and half a dozen school buses. Fees are 500 dollars per year, less for Hezbollah members—and free tuition for the children of martyrs.

❊

Despite the early reliance of Hezbollah-run schools like the Madrasa al-Mahdi on Iranian money, by the end of the 1990s Hezbollah had largely detached itself from its Iranian beginnings. Hardly any pictures of Khomeini hang in the streets of southern Lebanese Shi'ite towns anymore. Instead there are pictures of local heroes such as Musa Sadr, the charismatic leader of the Lebanese Shi'ites who disappeared in Libya in 1978, wearing the distant smile of a Giotto Madonna.

The handful of rag-tag "warriors of God" of the early days has been replaced by a small but highly trained army. The era when the Hezbollah fighters "ran up the hills, attacked enemy positions, shouted 'allahu akbar' and were shot dead" was already a thing of the past by the start of the 1990s, as local spokesman for the United Nations military force Timur Göksel puts it in his typically colorful manner.[36] Their training camps now feature classrooms in which soldier recruits learn ballistics, the science of explosives—and patience. These classrooms make it clear that suicide bombings, far from being the rash acts of desperate men, are sparingly used and carefully calculated operations, designed to generate the minimum number of martyrs and maximum effect.

Hezbollah's communications strategies and operations have become just as sophisticated. Its leadership understands that how the war is reported in the local and regional media is just as important as how it is fought. "The media are part of the war," says Malek Wabdeh, a Hezbollah cultural representative, "CNN is more important than airplanes."[37] Most Hezbollah commando troop missions and martyr operations are dispatched with a camera crew in tow. Footage of these operations is typically on air within hours of the attack. It is

73

a phenomenally successful form of martyr-marketing, conducted through the offices of Hezbollah's own television station, Manar TV.

Founded in the early 1990s, Manar Television's fare is varied, and at times decidedly grim. In the mornings, children's shows; sports in the afternoons; and, at prime time, an enemy tank flying through the air and shattering into pieces. This is Islamic reality television, and it routinely scores very high ratings.

Until 2000, Manar TV's headquarters was in a bunker complex beneath a sea of houses in southern Beirut. At the time of my first visit, in 1997, the station's offices had a very military feel, with its disguised entrance, radio interference on cell phones, and the low cellar passageways. On the inside the station functioned like a western-based professional media operation. By 1997, 120 people worked in this complex.

"At first, no one in Beirut wanted to believe it," recalls Galal Haj Hassan, one of Manar TV's program directors, "so we showed it. We had to show things like Israelis shot dead, exploding tanks, and martyrs because the Lebanese are very mistrustful and would never have believed us otherwise. Israelis never die, thought our *frères de la résistance*"—he uses the French expression deliberately, attempting to capture some of the mystique of the French resistance against the Nazis. "Why does the world portray us as terrorists?" he wonders. "How are we worse than the French resistance of fifty years ago?" He points out that his station attracts a significant Israeli audience. "Their military HQ watches all our stuff and we sell our material to Israeli channels too, via pools like Reuters TV." In the meantime, Manar TV is said to top the ratings in the south and in the Bekaa, with 800,000 viewers. With its mélange of Qur'an exegesis and cartoons, says Hassan proudly, Manar's children's TV is already "Number 1 in the entire country."

In 2000, Manar TV's growing success made it possible to move its headquarters from well-hidden cellars to a brand-new three-story building with a glass frontage and a large nameplate at the entrance. The station now produces six news broadcasts per day. Three chief editors rotate during the day, and permanent correspondents report back from Russia, Iran, Egypt, the Palestinian areas, France, and Washington. People can receive Al-Manar via satellite in Europe and the United States, and plans are afoot for further expansion, including English and Hebrew news broadcasts. Hebrew? "Why, certainly!" says Hussein Nabulsi from the PR department, enjoying the joke. "They watch us anyway. And we've got plenty of Hebrew-speaking announcers." Where did they learn their Hebrew? "Well, in Israeli prisons." We proceed past the Martyrs' Honor Board, listing cameramen who lost their lives on the job, and past the huge CD library with "Spectacular Sound Effects, Vol. II," to the room which one of the technicians calls their "war room": the editing room of the video department. This is where they also produce videos of the *istishhaadis,* the suicide bombers—in advance, of course: "there are films here of *istishhaadis* who, however, never become *istishhaadis.*" In other words, martyrs-in-waiting.

The stern face of Ayatollah Khomeini glows as a screensaver on a monitor in the editing room. On another screen, shrieking Arab men ride on horseback across a desert landscape. Culled by production editor Mustafa from the Hollywood film *Mohammed, Messenger of God,* starring Anthony Quinn, the images are intended to serve as a soundtrack to the next speech of Hezbollah's charismatic Secretary-General Sheikh Hassan Nasrallah. A Hollywood version of the conquering of Mecca? "Why not?" replies Mustafa, inserting yet another of his recent masterpieces into the video machine for my edification. This one features an earlier, inflammatory speech of Nasrallah, set to the soundtrack from the movie *Titanic.* It's a strange viewing experience. One sees and hears Nasrallah praise the martyrs and hold forth on the honor of fighting the traitors and the dignity of the heroic dead, while the music evokes the image of Leonardo DiCaprio, prepared to die for Kate Winslet in the freezing water. The editing is good: the pauses in Nasrallah's speech seem to match the beat of the pounding *Titanic* theme music. "Why shouldn't we combine them?" asks the technician from the throne of his ultramodern mixing desk, as he fiddles with the controls and looks up again. "*Titanic!* Downfall of hubris! It all fits wonderfully!" Why shouldn't they indeed, I think wearily. In a world of digitized media, everything can be combined and rearranged. If quotations from the Qur'an can be combined with Gandhi and Ho Chi Minh—as I have seen in other videos—why not have the musical motifs of *Titanic* pounding behind Nasrallah's words?

❖

It is common to think of Hezbollah more as an uncompromising religious movement than as a wheeling and dealing political party. In this vein, an Iranian journalist living in exile in Paris, Amir Taheri, predicted in 1986 that Hezbollah "would be very put out to be described as a political organization with political goals. Its religious leaders recruit members in the name of Islam. Their long-term aim is to convert—using violence if necessary—the whole of mankind to Muhammad's faith."[38]

But Taheri had got it wrong. Muhammad Ghat, Hezbollah party spokesman and former lecturer in philosophy, sees himself very much as a political force: "We view our declaration of loyalty to democracy as a strategic investment, for what kind of future would we have if we were opposed to democracy?" Of course they would like to see an Islamic state come into being, he said—as soon as a majority is in favor of it. "We want to change the political forms of the system—but not according to our own taste," insists Ghat. "*All* the Lebanese ought to be able to say yes to it." This position is not as selfless as it may seem at first glance. Since the Shi'ites are the fastest-growing group in the population and may well soon constitute the majority of the Lebanese, pious declarations in favor of majority rule are entirely in Hezbollah's favor.

Hezbollah's political savvy was strikingly demonstrated at a public rally in the small town of Bint Jbail, attended by thousands, just days after the hurried—some said panicky—retreat of the Israeli soldiers from their self-proclaimed "security zone" in southern Lebanon. The enemy's aura of invincibility had been shattered, and jubilant Hezbollah partisans in the crowd came to hear Hassan Hezbollah's Secretary-General, Sheikh Nasrallah, speak about the victory. Everyone ex-

pected him to announce that he now wanted to take the battle to Jerusalem. Instead, Nasrallah talked about roads, schools, hospitals;
about prudence and reconstruction; about infrastructure measures
and the power supply in Hermel, probably the country's poorest town
in the north of the Bekaa plains, where people now cultivated hashish
because the potato crop no longer earned enough money. Political
prudence seemed to be the order of the day, as the Hezbollah leadership deliberately pulled back from talk of total war to demonstrate its
concern for the social welfare of the people.

"Everyone had been afraid that the Israeli retreat would be followed
by a repeat of the usual Lebanese tragedy of the conquerors massacring
the conquered," explains Prime Minister Rafiq Hariri's economics ad-
visor Kamal Hamdane, who is working for the government on a reconstruction program for the south. "But nothing of the sort happened.
Hezbollah has very responsibly avoided any further bloodshed. It's a cu-
rious thing, but it seems to be the first religious movement in Lebanese
history to have grasped that we are sick of minor religious wars."

Circumspect to the point of invisibility, Hezbollah now controls
southern Lebanon. Its leaders pull all the strings with great aplomb in
the villages and clans; negotiate with Christian peasants and priests; and
tactfully look the other way as Christian-operated supermarkets sell
whiskey. They deal carefully with the collaborators of yore. Although
the yellow Hezbollah banners in the shape of a Kalashnikov still fly
above villages and roads, the fighters have seemingly vanished. The
highly organized little fighting force has—for the time being—turned
itself back into hundreds of farmers, shopkeepers, and wage earners.

Twenty years after the first Hezbollah suicide attack in Tyre, the "psychological atom bomb"[39] of the weak against the powerful has pro-
liferated like a virus. It flourishes in all sorts of diverse societies and
has given terrorism a whole new dimension. In Lebanon, "the devel-
opmental laboratory" of the modern martyr, though, enthusiasm for
suicide attacks has waned. "If we hadn't had [the suicide bombers],

we wouldn't have been able to win," Sheikh Fadlallah was already saying in 2000, "but we don't need them any more." The readiness of people to die has been fundamentally proven; and the myth continues to exist. But revealingly, Fadlallah, *spiritus rector* of the most radical of Lebanese Shi'ites, was one of the first high-ranking Islamic scholars to publicly condemn the September 11 attacks. "Nothing can justify the murder of thousands of innocent civilians. No religion justifies such a thing. The Islamic resistance in Lebanon has never killed civilians. All those who were killed were Israeli soldiers!"[40] Even as people on the streets in Egypt and Saudi Arabia, America's closest allies in the Arab world, give vent to their hatred for the United States, Hezbollah leader Nasrallah now warns his people against believing that disagreements with the Americans can be attributed to a religious war pitting Islam against Christianity: "That's a trap."[41]

Hezbollah's early use of suicide attacks fits well with the Shi'ite tradition of "victimhood." But the Shi'ites of southern Lebanon are tired of being victims, and want to shed the stigma of impotence. Thus the Ashura festivals have been massively scaled back in Lebanese towns and villages due to Hezbollah pressure.[42] A culture of victory, of winners, seems more attractive than a culture of victimhood—and Hezbollah regards itself as the victor. Hezbollah party members often and loudly pledge solidarity to the Palestine cause. But Nasrallah also counsels them more quietly to stop stylizing themselves as eternal victims.

By the beginning of 2002, the idea of dispatching a suicide bomber on his final journey every couple of days meets with head-shaking and concern among the Hezbollah leadership. That, says one of their functionaries, would be a suicidal waste of a life: "You have to treat something as special as a martyr operation very carefully. Human lives are precious after all!"

Israel and Palestine

THE CULTURE OF DEATH

✦

The bodies of the exploding martyrs smell of musk.
—Hamas functionary from Gaza

The worst thing is when someone blows himself up in a bus:
it takes weeks for you to escape from the smell of petrol and
burnt flesh. And you can never forget it.
—Yonatan Yagodovsky, Jerusalem manager of *Magen David Adom,*
the Israeli Red Cross

It happens yet again: the dry "ker-boom!" of a detonation, and then another. The sound of the blast continues to hang in the air for a moment before everything goes so quiet it seems as if the explosion had carried all sound away with it. Once again people, torn apart and dying, lie between burst tires, bent metal parts, and entire sheets of bodywork, all covered with shards of glass. And once again it's less than a minute before one hears the first police and ambulance sirens; first one, then another, then dozens of them all over the city—a noise so loud and unmistakable that even residents of outlying suburbs immediately know what has happened.

Motzei Shabbat is the Hebrew name for this time of day: it's the evening after the Sabbath, when cafés reopen, buses start running again, and life in general begins to pick up its pace. Young people meet, flirt, stroll, and drink. In Jerusalem, the favorite meeting place is Ben Yehuda Street, the pedestrian precinct in the city center. It was precisely here, on the evening of Saturday, November 30, 2001, half an hour before midnight, the time when the largest number of night owls are out and about, that Osama Bahar and Nabil Abu Halabiya blew up themselves and ten other people.

The aftermath of the blast follows a depressingly familiar routine. As usual, within seconds of receiving the news, the head of operations for Magen David Adom alerts hundreds of first aid workers and volunteers who have learned to keep their rescue equipment ready and waiting in their cars. All access to the area is blocked off, in case of another explosive charge that hasn't yet been detonated—which in fact there is in this case: it explodes in a neighboring street, shown live on television by the Israeli camera crews.

Once again, the police try to take fingerprints of the suspected perpetrators—one of the only ways of verifying their identity, as there's not much left to work with except fingers, feet, and heads. Orthodox Jewish men belonging to the *Hevra Kadisha,* the burial society, slip yellow jackets over their black cloaks to identify themselves as members of the salvage team. Their job is to gather up the torn limbs, internal organs, fingers, teeth, and other small body parts so that the victims' families at least have some pieces to bury later on.

Parents begin calling the hospitals' emergency wards before dialing the last, dreaded phone number: that of the forensic institute in Abu Kabir, south of Tel Aviv. This is the end of the line, where a small team of forensic scientists, doctors, and psychologists typically work for twenty-four or forty-eight hours non-stop to establish as quickly as possible the identities of those who died. Orthopedic surgeons, dentists, radiologists once again brace themselves for a nocturnal phone call from Abu Kabir, asking whether so-and-so was one of their patients; whether they might be able to dig out dental charts, x-ray images, to help identify the victims.

But the dreary routine doesn't stop there. Once again, Israel's air force scrambles its fighter jets, and bombs Palestinian police stations and military quarters, and Israeli tanks advance into Gaza, Nablus,

Ramallah, and Jenin. Palestinians, once again, will be killed, which provokes Hamas and the smaller "Islamic Jihad" group to swear revenge, and eventually, to make good on their threats, despite all the precautions taken by Israeli security forces.

After just a few hours, Israeli society, as it usually does in the wake of such an attack, carries on as if nothing had happened. The debris is removed, and the officials from the state compensation board duly notified. Three days after the attack of November 30, 2001, at the spot where it all happened, directly opposite the Café Chagall, with its bulging, scarred, shattered facade, a new, glossy poster is mounted in front of the police barricades announcing a massive "Gay and Lesbian Night" for the coming Sunday evening, complete with drag show and featuring the popular local dj Magji. Around the corner, on Ben Yehuda Street itself and only five meters away from Chagall, a two-story stage tent is being set up for the concert, where sound and lighting technicians are testing the equipment. Isn't it dangerous to put on a concert now, I ask them? "It's precisely now," replies one of the techies, busying himself further with five cables, "that we have to carry on, to carry on celebrating"—as if open-air concerts and dancing through the night were expressions of victory over terror.

Israel's citizens have become besieged in their own country. Fear dominates public spaces—cafés, streets, buses, and discos. No one knows who'll be hit next, or where the next attack will come from. Attackers can strike anywhere that people congregate. The country's overall mood is one of disappointment, bitterness, and anger—but mostly of exhaustion. In a country whose inhabitants were previously total news junkies, many now only watch or listen to the news if they have to. It's just too much to witness the endless loop of televised image after image of blown-up buses, ambulances racing from the scene, and new families standing at freshly dug graves, trying to stop one another from collapsing.

Pizza deliveries and video rentals are booming, since many Israelis are afraid to leave their homes. Invitations to parties include notes intended to reassure invitees that armed guards will be present. School-age children don't have to ask their parents for cell phones, as the phones are practically forced upon them so their parents can always find out where their offspring are.

The country's exhaustion has fed a growing appetite for escapism. A summer 2001 weekend edition of the daily paper *Ha'aretz* was already listing "fifty ways to escape from reality," including everything from emigration to drugs to trips to India. The tourist charter flight business is booming. Cheap flights to Europe are advertised everywhere: skiing in Italy, New Year in Paris; spring in Amsterdam, Thailand at any time—whatever you do, just don't stay at home. And "so far as hashish, marijuana, and ecstasy are concerned," reckons Shlomo Gal, director of the Israeli Anti-Drug Authority, "our country has meanwhile become comparable to Amsterdam and New York."[1]

The country is exhausted, yes, but there is another pervasive, understated sentiment that Israel's political and military elites would never admit to: a feeling of helplessness, of impotence. It was manifest in the tearful lament of a police officer at the joint funeral of two Russian-born Israeli teenage girls, who perished along with nineteen others in a June 2001 suicide attack on a Tel Aviv nightclub. Trembling with rage, the red-eyed officer at first declared that all Palestinian terrorists should be killed. Then he paused abruptly, and started weeping again. "What are we supposed to do, then?" he almost shouts. "Threaten to shoot him if he blows himself up? All he does is laugh, and press his button! What are we supposed to do?"[2]

***

The suicide attack of November 30, 2001 was the first in more than two and a half months. Since September 11, Hamas and the other main Palestinian paramilitary group, Islamic Jihad, had refrained from sending out living bombs. Although gun battles between Palestinian militia and Israeli soldiers continued unabated, U.S. President Bush's sudden recognition of the Palestinians' right to their own state—accorded when he was gathering allies for the global coalition against terrorism—stopped the momentum of the suicide attacks for a while. But after the American military victory against the Taliban in

Afghanistan, as Bush's appeal for Palestinian self-determination seemed to lose its urgency, the Israeli government of Prime Minister Ariel Sharon had free rein once again. On November 23, in another of Israel's series of "preventative liquidations" of avowed enemies, a rocket fired by an Israeli helicopter commando killed Mahmud Abu Hanud, the legendary Hamas leader from Nablus. Hamas swore retaliation. As if to make a mockery of the Israeli security measures sealing off Gaza and the West Bank, the Café Chagall attackers of November 30 came this time from Abu Dis, a suburb of Jerusalem under complete Israeli control.

Around 125 miles further southwest of Jerusalem in the Gaza Strip, sounds of delight erupted in the hours following the November 30 attack. In Abu Mustafa's half-open tent, on thin foam mattresses laid out for the evening get-together of the men from the refugee camp Khan Yunis, people are laughing. Cell phones ring, and casualty figures are bandied about. That's what seems to count the most: the figures. How many did the bombers take with them? The victims are treated with no sympathy, the attackers with the greatest possible pride. "Our lives are that cheap, you know," says one man who had narrowly missed being shot dead days earlier when his taxi came under fire from an Israeli position. But how, I asked, could you support women and children being killed too? "The Israelis kill our women and children. We're at war here: innocent people get hit." Children and soldiers: isn't there a difference between them? Yes, no . . . the company is undecided. The voices of the men become louder, and they smoke ceaselessly. From time to time, someone calls to ask about a friend or family member who is seriously injured—"Mahmud, is everything okay? They said he was in hospital . . ."—then my taxi driver acquaintance turns round again, saying: "Children? No, they're not a target." Another one adds: "Children of settlers are okay, but *mish hadifi*, not the target." The names of killed Palestinian children are reeled off and, finally, he says: "The person who goes on the mission chooses the target. It's his decision."

Suddenly the thirteen men in Mustafa's tent start singing and clapping to the simple melody of a "martyr song": "You gave us the courage to become martyrs. You teach us to live united." When the singing dies down, agrarian engineer Kamal Aqeel—at fifty-one, the oldest man at this gathering—starts speaking, and everyone quiets down. "Believe me, I mourn for every drop of blood that is shed. We know what suffering and bloodshed mean. But just look at the son of a typical worker: he watches how his father is insulted and turned away at the checkpoint. He asks: where is my uncle? Dead. Where is my brother? In jail. Every child here is fed on anger—they suck it in with their mother's milk—and at some point the pressure just becomes unbearable."

Aqeel is acting mayor of Khan Yunis. In his three-piece suit, he could pass for a company CEO. He spent years in Israeli prisons and, in the mid-1990s, was one of the leading peace activists in the Gaza Strip. His is a typical Palestinian biography. "In 1996, practically all of us were still against the martyr operations. Not any longer. I was against it; we were in the middle of the peace process and thought: let's give peace a chance. Society was against it then, and the *sulta*" (the "power," a term typically used here to refer to Yasser Arafat's Palestinian Authority) "really tried to destroy the groups and arrest their men. Now the whole situation is different. Now people are just longing for the next operation! We all feel that we can no longer bear the situation as it is; we feel that we'd simply explode under all this pressure of humiliation. They're doing it for us."

Aqeel recalls how "in 1994, after seven years of intifada, people laid olive branches on the Jeeps of the departing Israeli troops." At that time, he received delegations of Israelis who had lost their sons in Gaza—"lovely people—we never had a problem with them." But then came the brutal encounters with soldiers and settlers, the collapse of peace negotiations, the loss of jobs in Israel—and, eventually, the abandonment of all hope. To illustrate the situation of his people, Aqeel launches into a joke. Bush, Arafat, and Sharon find themselves in Hell. Bush wants to call home and is allowed to, but has to pay 1,000 U.S. dollars for ten lousy minutes. Sharon, likewise, pays through the nose for only a few minutes. They both accept this with some mumbling and grumbling—but when they see Yasser Arafat sitting in a corner and evidently spending hours on the phone with friends and comrades in arms, they kick up a real stink with the devil in charge. How does he manage that? complain the ex–heads of state. "It's quite simple," replies the devil. "Arafat's calling at local rate!"

Aqeel's niece Hadil,[3] a journalist and translator, leads me to the house of another family in the Khan Yunis refugee camp. They fled to this camp in 1948, in the south of the Gaza Strip, where the sea is beyond even this distant horizon. Down the road is Gush Katif, one of nineteen Israeli settlements in the Gaza Strip which collectively take up about a third of Gaza's land mass and consume about a third of its scarce water supply—all for the use of approximately 6,000 settlers. One million Palestinians, or possibly even 1.2 million—census figures are unreliable—live on Gaza's remaining 230 square miles.

As Hadil and I sit and talk on a tiny terrace, we hear heavy machine-gun fire erupt from Gush Katif. Salvos ring out for half an hour, followed by sporadic individual shots. "They're ours," says Aqeel, looking up to the heavens like a farmer looking at the clouds for signs of rain. He makes a beckoning gesture with his hand. "Please go inside. Ricochets and splinters sometimes land here"—for there are only six rows of houses separating us from the shell-ravaged, shifting edge of Khan Yunis. Minutes later, the news whizzes from house to house: thirteen-year-old Muhammad Sanadiq has been shot dead. That was what the noise of the machine guns was all about. The slightly built child had a toy pistol in his hand, and got too close to the stretch of no-man's land.

As a precaution, all the young men make themselves scarce from the houses at the edge of the camp and onlookers park themselves on the roofs while the shooting continues from Gush Katif's concrete towers. In the last few months, says Hadil, these gun battles have always been a prelude to an Israeli army sortie. This time is no different. Tanks suddenly appear, and bulldozers flatten another row of houses at the edge of Khan Yunis—another few dozen people will resort to living in the round tents. Houses on the side of the refugee camp closest to the settlement are most at risk. Five rows of these houses have disappeared since summer 2001, as the boundaries of

Gush Katif seem to creep ever closer. Soon the Aqeel family's home may be at risk, forcing them to flee as they did once before, in 1948.

"They drove us out once before—and now they're driving us out of the refugee camps. That really is a step too far," says Kamal Aqeel. "We lose something every day: we've lost the land, the sea, and our freedom: it's just not acceptable." Both sides, the Israelis and the Palestinian Authority alike, had, he said, destroyed all hope. "Arafat? Oh, Arafat! He let himself get mixed up in negotiations with the Israelis—and he lost. After all, he's done everything they wanted: he arrested his own countrymen, had them shot, and what did he get in return? His own circle has become rich, but we've gained nothing—nothing!"

I spend days traveling around Khan Yunis, trying to find families of recent suicide bombers and those who recruit them. One evening I find myself in a taxi driving through a wild proliferation of ramshackle houses on streets which don't appear on any map. I am taken to a calm and friendly young man who introduces himself as "quite an authority on Hamas." He gives his name as Wardan and declares politely but firmly that he wants to set one thing straight right from the start. There are no suicide bombers here; the very term was wrong. These are "holy explosions," and the attackers themselves are "human dynamite"—as if the human being himself were a weapon; as if the bomb round his waist made him a human rocket. "We don't have tanks or F-16 jets. But we have something better: our exploding Islamic bombs. All they cost is our lives, but nothing can beat them—not even nuclear weapons!"

Such people weren't suicide bombers, he explained patiently, but *shahids,* martyrs. Even more than that: they're *istishhaadis,* the very essence of a martyr—a "top shaheed" is someone worth even more than a soldier shot dead in battle. And what, I ask, would you think of someone who just does away with himself in his private home out of sheer desperation—in other words, someone who commits suicide? I get an uncomprehending look in response. "Pff . . . you don't do that. That would be *haram,* an action that goes against God's commandments!"

Wardan abruptly changes the subject and begins talking about the appropriate tactics for martyr operations. "Around ten operations failed because the men weren't walking properly. They were too quick, too anxious; they were in too much a hurry. Apart from that, their disguise was perfect: some were wearing army uniforms; others were clean shaven; others wore earrings or wigs and the gear of the ultra-orthodox. But no one dressed like that would normally rush around nervously." In the mid-to-late–1990s, when the human bombs were men who were still allowed into Israel proper on work permits, the *istishhaadis* would have been familiar with the places they were going to attack. Now they are much more likely to be arriving in Tel Aviv for the first time in their lives. Wardan insists, nevertheless, that they are less likely than ever to be discovered: "Earlier, it took a long time to prepare a martyr, and their families weren't allowed to know anything about it." Nowadays, on the contrary, it all happens much faster. The more hopeless the situation becomes, and the larger the number of people who have gone before, the more quickly the next lot are ready. "All of us here fear nothing more except God. Either our jihad is successful and we achieve liberation, or we'll enter Paradise as martyrs." But death? No, honestly—"we love death just as much as the Jews fear it. For this is the only thing our enemies are afraid of!"

Human bombs are cheap: all you need—apart from the will to sacrifice yourself—are nails, an explosive, a battery, a switch, a short bit of cable, a couple of chemicals, and a sturdy belt with large compartments. The most expensive thing, says Wardan, is the taxi journey to some remote Israeli town, often involving secret routes in order to circumvent the checkpoints. Once the deed has been done, the sponsoring organization pays for the memorial service and the burial and, at the end of it all, makes a lump-sum payment of $300 to $500 to the family.[4]

The suicide assassin typically records a video testament in advance of the bombing. Flanked by a Kalashnikov and the Qur'an, and with the organization's banner behind him, he reads out his testament and talks about the motives behind his actions: we hear about Palestine, freedom, the Paradise where he will see the other martyrs again—and that it's God's will. Does he mention revenge, too? I ask Wardan. "No," replies the man from Hamas, "it has no more to do with private revenge than it has to do with suicide. If revenge were the only motivating factor, his martyrdom would be sullied in the eyes of God. It's a military action. The candidate watches his predecessors' videos over and over again, and watches his own, too, in order to rid himself of any fear. He familiarizes himself with what he's about to do. Then he can greet death like an old friend."

The bomber, continues Wardan, ties up all his personal affairs during his last days. If he owes anyone money, he pays off his debts. He spends his last night praying. Before setting off on the mission, he carries out the kind of washing ritual that precedes prayer; he puts clean clothes on; shaves; and takes part in communal prayers in the mosque one last time. He will ask God for forgiveness for all his sins for one final time. Then he puts a small Qur'an in his left breast pocket and straps on his explosive burden. It's the same routine tried and tested dozens of times before. None of his family knows what he's planning to do. Even within Hamas, the sponsoring organization, very few know of the individual's involvement or plans, for the groups preparing for attacks are divided up into tiny cells called *unqud*, "bunches of grapes," whose cadres only know the members of their own cell.

As soon as the bomber has fulfilled his murderous mission, the organization in whose name he has acted distributes copies of the videocassette to the news media. His deed becomes a great topic of conversation in the mosques, new fodder for posters, graffiti, and videos. Al-Manar, the Hezbollah satellite channel from Beirut, often shows scenes from the farewell video along with TV pictures of the scene of the bombing, all set to "martyr songs."

Ismail Masawabi, one of the *istishhaadis* from Khan Yunis, who blew himself up on June 22, 2001 at the edge of the neighboring Israeli settlement, can be taken as an example. He donned a kippa, the traditional Jewish head-covering for men, and drove his car towards the gate of the settlement, but got stuck in the sand. When two soldiers appeared, he called for help in Hebrew. They thought he was a settler, and when they approached the car to offer assistance, Ismail pressed the detonator, thereby becoming a martyr—a hero. His family's entire living room was henceforth turned into an Ismail shrine. Photo collages decorate the walls. As I sit in this living room shrine, one of the hero's cousins energetically defends Ismail's actions. "Anyone with an atom of honor in his body should do it," he says heatedly. Everyone in the room chimes in immediately in assent—except for Ismail's father, who sits quietly. For seconds that seem to last forever, he sits silently beneath all the pictures of his son the hero, and it seems as if he's gradually shrinking, sinking into the sofa. Finally, he clears his throat, and says quietly, "and I bought him everything he needed—a computer, a camera, even a car."

Why Ismail? Why the son of a wealthy window manufacturer who provided for his family's every need? Why such a talented landscape painter and calligrapher who had taken commissions for lettering, and had even painted the surahs of the Qur'an in the hall of the mosque opposite? The same Ismail who, just before his college exams, and weeks before his end, was standing in this same living room, promising to bring home decent grades? (His father understood the fatal word-play only afterwards, for *shuhada* means "grades"—but also "martyrdom.")

Weeks before his mission, Ismail's sister had come across the kippa he would don for the attack among his things, but had thought it was one of his theatre props—Ismail acted in a small amateur group. Then he disappeared at dawn. "We planned to open the shop downstairs for his painting," says his father. "We went to Kufa in Iraq and brought painting materials back with us—he'd have got commissions straight away." For a moment, he loses his composure. "That was what I hoped. But at least"—and here he clears his throat again—"we're happy that he died in this way—that he didn't die at home, that he wasn't just shot dead at the checkpoint." His last will and testament, says his mother, all seven densely packed sheets of it, won first prize at the university. (Apparently the Islamic universities in Gaza have so many martyr alumni in their classes that one of the lecturers established a competition for the best written testament.) The document is hanging up next to the pictures.

What follows is taken from the "official" version of Ismail's testament—the document that won first prize, that was meant for publication. Ismail also left behind a second, private testament for his family, which is reproduced below, following the first. The family is happy to show off a copy of the public document, but when I ask about the private one, they hesitate. In the end, however, they send Ismail's youngest brother off to the little copy shop to make copies of both documents for me. What the two documents reveal, essentially, are two views of a murderer and suicide.

> Thanks be to God who brings about the mujahideens' victory and the dictators' defeat, and praise be to Muhammad, the faithful, honorable Prophet Muhammad, and all his friends, and all those who have followed in his footsteps.
>
> Dear Muslim youth the world over: I greet you with the blessed greetings of Islam; greetings that I send to all of you who fight in the name of religion and the nation; greetings to all those who are convinced fighters and martyrs.
>
> Dear Muslim youth: I wish to let you know that I hold those of you in particularly high regard who were always first to come to the mosque for prayers.
>
> Dear brothers: there is no doubt about the situation prevailing in the Muslim Umma, the Muslim nation. This situation is clear to everyone, old and young. It's a situation that makes us weep and makes our hearts ache because of what has happened to the Muslims. We are truly grieved about it.
>
> Before we had power, then we became weak. We live in humiliation, where we once lived in dignity. We are ignorant where we were once wise. We are now bringing up the world's rear, where we were once its leaders.

The wish to become a martyr dominates my life, my heart, my soul and my feelings. When I hear the Qur'an's verses I become sad because I'm doing nothing to change the situation. . . . Our nation has become so weak, and people just help themselves to whatever they want. We are a nation living in disgrace and under Jewish occupation. This happened to us because we didn't fight them; we didn't fight for God.

I reject this terrible and dark situation which I know and experience, and I have decided to become a shining light, illuminating the way for all Muslims—and a blazing fire to burn to death the enemy of God. Just standing there and watching our Muslim people being slaughtered [by the Jews] and not taking any action to change the situation is a dirty game that I will not tolerate. . . . Therefore, in the name of Jerusalem and the Al Aqsa Mosque, in the name of God on earth, I prefer to meet God and leave humankind behind. Therefore I have told myself that I will be with the Prophet Muhammad and his followers tomorrow. . . .

God will not forgive you if you accept such a life. The alternative is the true life. God will not forgive you if you accept humiliation and don't fight to put an end to the situation and to strengthen Islam.

My brothers and my family: I shall be in Paradise, where everything will be mine. So don't be sad that you've lost me. In Paradise I shall be immortal, so you should be glad that I'm there. To all those who have loved me, I say: don't weep, for your tears won't give me peace. This is the way I have chosen. So, if you have really loved me, carry on and carry my weapon.

I have decided to take up arms and follow the brigade of Izz al-Din al-Qassam martyrs in order to make the Jews feel some of the suffering and devastation they subject my people to every day, and have subjected them to for a long time.

Greetings from a martyr who wishes to see you all again one day in the Paradise of God, the creator of heaven and earth. Greetings to everyone who knew and loved me, and who loves the way of the jihad and the mujahideen.

I hope that God accepts me as a martyr.

From the testament for his family:

Dear Mama, dear Papa,

You who have taken such trouble with my upbringing; you who woke at night in order that I might rest and sleep; you who brought me up as a Muslim: you are as dear to me as my eyes and my heart. You did your very best to turn me into an adult human. You helped me enormously, and may Allah reward you for it in the best possible manner. I can't find the right words to thank you for everything you've done for me, but I ask God the Almighty to reunite us in Paradise.

My beloved parents, I know that it's hard and difficult for you to lose me, but don't forget that we'll see each other in Paradise. This is God's promise. What a wonderful and lovely promise if we all see each other again there.

Dear Mama: be patient and happy and pray to God to thank him for giving you a martyr as a son. And think of al-Khansaa,[5] who gave her four sons as martyrs for God because she knew they would all meet again in Paradise and that she would also get there one day, too.

Dear, good father: please forgive me. Forgive me for not fulfilling your dream of seeing me complete my university studies and of being proud of me for getting a job. But you should be content. Your son will not, it is true, receive the *Shihada*[6]—but will instead receive the great *Sha-hada*.[7] You should be proud of that.

You are the one who taught me to be a man in every situation. You are the one who raised a lion in his house, who taught the enemies of God and the Muslims fear. Forgive me, dear father, if you are surprised to receive the news of my martyrdom, for I know that you're just waiting for me to finish my studies any day now—but this is what I have to do in the present situation. And we will see each other in another life.

My beloved brothers: I have loved you from the bottom of my heart. Be good to father and mother.

My dear fellow believers, dear Muhammad, Ahmed, and Mahmud, you are the youth of the future. When I am dead, please be good to my parents. Help my father with his work, and my mother at home. And go to the Mosque regularly. Don't make bad friends. Read the Qur'an.

My beloved, good sisters: I was always happy to see you and to talk to you. When I visited you, you welcomed me with a friendly smile and warm words. Be patient and thank God, and please forgive me if I have made a mistake."

Ismail's picture is plastered all over the walls of Khan Yunis, along with pictures of dozens of other martyrs. The posters are often pasted on top of one another, and between them are posters of green birds flying up into a crimson sky, the martyrs' souls in the color of the Prophet, winging their way to Paradise.

"We live in a culture of death," says Hadil, as we leave Ismail's family's house. "And besides: where's the difference for the kids if they get shot dead even when they chuck stones?" Later on, when Hadil's niece is sitting at the dining room table and saying, in her little girl's voice, "I'd like to be a martyr," Hadil becomes furious. "She's eight, damn it. D'you get it? *Eight!*" Of the two hundred Palestinian children who, according to UNESCO, have died in Israeli army fire since September 2000, fifty were from Khan Yunis. Children residing in this camp place themselves in grave peril by playing, loitering, or causing mischief in the wreckage of the bombed-out homes on the western side of Khan Yunis—the side closest to the Israeli settlement. The afternoons are especially bad. "Why afternoons?" I ask. "Because that's when the shooting starts." Taxi drivers now carefully avoid the last hundred yards before the rubble starts, since a driver was shot dead there in autumn. Only the children keep on coming to the area, throwing stones and daring each other to stand there at all. The Palestinian photographer Abed saw two of them die: "One of them was bending down to pick up a stone, no bigger than a pebble. Two seconds later he was dead. The other one waved his hands at the Israeli sentry and called 'yoo-hoo!' Those were his last movements."

The Israeli soldier who pulled the trigger has little reason to fear sanctions. Even when, in December 2001, a mine freshly buried on a school route blew up five children from the same family, who had been walking home from school, the army leadership simply reprimanded those responsible for their "bad choice" of location. Hadil who, like her uncle, maintains that she had been a pacifist, says "They kill us, we kill them. End of story!"

Charismatic but sober-minded, Dr. Khalil Shikaki is sitting on a black leather sofa on a beige carpet in front of a little gallery of photos showing him with Senator Edward Kennedy and other prominent figures. After a distinguished career in half a dozen universities in the United States, Kuwait, and Bahrain, he returned to the West Bank in the wake of the Oslo Peace Accords, and founded the first Palestinian Center for Policy and Survey Research in Nablus, later setting up a new one in Ramallah after internal disputes. He's every inch the elegant scholar, holding forth over tea and candied fruits, on the perception of threats and cost-benefit analyses—all the while focusing on a single topic: which sort of Palestinian is likely to blow him- or herself up with a couple of kilograms of TNT strapped to the waist, when is he or she likely to do it, and what percentage of the Palestinian population in the occupied territories approves of it.

Adopting a measured, dispassionate tone and concerned with maintaining clarity, Shikaki tries to explain the phenomenon as if he were a scientist on the trail of a menacing epidemic. He's serious, unlike his brother Fathi, who was a pediatrician by training and who enjoyed a laugh. The same eyes, the same mouth, the same powerful build, the same cropped ten-day-old beard and trendy, designer eyeglasses: the two brothers could scarcely have looked more alike. And yet these men, two of five sons of a refugee family from Gaza, could not have been more different. In their two biographies, we see the profound divisions among Palestinians in microcosm. Fathi, the older of the two, was one of the founders of a political faction whose actions the younger brother now researches in such painstaking detail. Fathi, head of Islamic Jihad, the ultra-radical Islamist group, was shot dead on the island of Malta in 1995 by agents of Mossad, Israel's intelligence service—nine months after he had sent a suicide commando mission into northern Tel Aviv which blew up twenty-one Israelis and catapulted Islamic Jihad into the premier league of Palestinian terrorist groups.

This is the history of one family. But the Shikakis' history, the story of old Ibrahim and his eight children, is also the history of the last half century in which the Palestinian people became what they are today because they had lost what had been theirs as a matter of course— their country, the freedom to move around it at will, and the dignity that came from deciding its destiny.

In 1947 the Arab nations and powers rejected the UN plan for dividing up Palestine, which was still under British mandate rule. When Israel declared its independence in the following spring, five neighboring Arab countries launched an attack. When the fighting was over, Israel occupied far more territory than what was alloted to it under the original plan, and 700,000 people, half the Arab population of that region, had either fled or been driven out.

One of the many who fled was the patriarch of the Shikaki family, Ibrahim. In 1998, when such things were still possible, Ibrahim agreed to make an excursion to Israel proper—to the very village from which he fled half a century before. At first, he felt a bit lost among the broad streets, the bowling alley, and the Toyota showroom on Menachem Begin Avenue in the small Israeli town of Rehovot. But despite his seventy years, he could still remember his first twenty years of life spent in what was then the Arab village of Zarnuga. Not much remains of the past—but a few things are still the same. "Turn right," he says, "this is the way to get to the mosque." You can still go down there, a long and dusty side-road to a ruined building that's all fenced in, and that now has a Star of David on the blue door.

This is where Ibrahim came as a boy to pray and hear the stories and sermons that his father, the imam of Zarnuga's mosque, used to read. The old mulberry tree is still standing; a few houses have remained. This had been the land of generations of Shikakis, planted with grain, orange and apricot trees, and cucumber vines. In May 1948, the Shikaki family had fled from the battles and the rumors of massacres of Palestinian civilians by Israeli troops, assuming they would be away for only a short while. But they were never allowed to return, and were forced to settle in the wasteland of the southern Gaza Strip where the refugee camp Rafah sprang up with nothing beyond it but sand and the Egyptian border.

It would take two decades and another devastating defeat in the Six-Day War of 1967 before radical Palestinians, under Yasser Arafat's leadership, changed the Palestinian Liberation Organization from a powerless debating society into either a terrorist group or a liberation movement, depending on your political perspective; a group which, with its guerrilla attacks, airplane hijackings, and bombings, forced the world to sit up and take notice.

Just as world public opinion was divided between those who saw Israelis as the oppressors of Palestinians and those who sympathized profoundly with an oppressed people who had finally found a home after the Holocaust, so too Ibrahim Shikaki's eight children were divided about what was right. Among the eight children raised in this family was a future, brilliant advocate of a democratic Palestine co-existing peacefully with Israel, as well as one of the founders of Islamic Jihad, whose main goal is the destruction of the Jewish state and its replacement with a Palestine based on Islamic principles.

Fathi Shikaki was born in 1951 in Rafah. The bright little infant quickly turned into a highly talented schoolboy. Encouraged by his illiterate mother, he successfully applied for a grant to study medicine at Cairo, and became a pediatrician. There was initially nothing to suggest that he would later cite Ayatollah Khomeini as his role model and praise the "human bombs." But it was at the Kazic University in Cairo that Islamic Jihad, with its strange redundant name (what's a jihad supposed to be if not Islamic?), was founded by Fathi Shikaki and other Islamists such as Abdul-Aziz Odeh.[8]

Fathi grew up in a world of rising radical Islamistic movements which, while not going totally unnoticed by Israel, were not yet viewed as especially dangerous. By the end of the 1980s, Fathi Shikaki defended a practice he called "extraordinary martyrdom" in a book entitled *Jihad fis sabil Allah* ("Jihad in the path of God"), claiming that "we can't achieve our aims with these operations if our mujahideen, our fighters, are incapable of causing an explosion within a matter of seconds, that cannot be prevented by our enemy. We can achieve our aims by causing an explosion which gives the mujahid no chance to hesitate or to escape. This would enable him to carry out a successful operation in the name of the jihad and the faith, destroy the enemy's morale, and sow the seeds of fear in the enemy's people." This capacity, "a gift from God," concluded Fathi, was put into practice some five years after the appearance of his book, when, in 1993, the first Palestinian suicide bomber appeared on the scene.

In 1988, Fathi Shikaki was deported from his home in Gaza and thereafter operated mainly from Damascus, gradually rising to the top of the Islamic Jihad organizational chart. Those who knew him claimed that Fathi was a charismatic, warm-hearted, and humorous man. "The room filled up if he came in," recalls a friend. Fathi, they all say, was an eloquent, clever theoretician who was one of the first to adopt Islam's renaissance as a model for the Palestinian struggle for independence and to recommend Khomeini's Iranian revolution as a model for the Arab world, notwithstanding all the differences of faith and history.[9]

Khalil Shikaki, several years his junior, remains one of the most articulate and forthright critics and analysts of Palestinian Islamism. He's a man who rejects violence and maintains ties with Israeli social scientists, despite having had his Ramallah-based office shot to pieces by Israeli troops. "I always thought Fathi's way was wrong," he tells me. "The important thing for my brother, at the end of the day, was for the battle to go on forever—and if I fear anything, it's that current developments might appear to prove him right, even though it would be a terrible cul-de-sac."

In 1993, when the peace process first got under way and while Khalil Shikaki was preparing for his return to Palestine, Fathi was sitting alone in Damascus, pondering his political future. It did not look especially bright in the immediate wake of the Oslo Peace Accords, which brought about a dramatic shift in the situation in Gaza and the West Bank. Arafat's forthcoming return from exile and international recognition of his Palestinian Authority changed the political map overnight. Above all, Hamas, the largest Islamist movement, which had grown steadily more powerful since its founding in 1988, was now doubly weakened. It suddenly found itself confronted by a secular leadership that had been fully recognized under international law. At the same time, it was losing popular support, as people viewed peace as having more to offer than mere resistance.

Ironically enough, it was Israel itself that had given Hamas a leg up in its earliest years. Israeli intelligence made a conscious decision to build up Islamist groups as a counterbalance to the PLO and, thus, to weaken Arafat and deepen the rift within Palestinian society. While it is difficult to imagine nowadays how the bearded men of Hamas could ever have been Israeli collaborators, the fact remains that the only Palestinian social organization to which the Israeli government ever granted a degree of latitude in the years before the Oslo Accords was Hamas.[10] The Defence Ministry gave the green light to Islamic institutions such as the Islamic University of Gaza, which would later become a backbone of the militants.[11] And when, in the 1980s, the ultra-faithful Islamist cadres stormed Gaza's few cinemas, set fire to the beachside restaurants for selling alcohol, and generally intimidated the public, Israeli soldiers just stood and watched. Only years later would they realize that, in so doing, they were nurturing their future—and, relative to the PLO, far more deadly—enemy.

Hamas was established in 1988, one year after the first intifada (Palestinian uprising) had broken out in Gaza and had spread to the West Bank. Palestinian Islamists neither wanted to place themselves under the Arafat-dominated "United Command" that had quickly taken hold of the uprising, nor stand on the sidelines as passive observers. On February 11, 1988, they published their first pamphlet of slogans in support of the intifada and, from that summer onwards, signed off as "Hamas"—an acronym for *Hakara al-Muqawama al-*

Islamyia, or Islamic Defense Movement, as well as a word meaning something along the lines of "élan" or "zeal."

Proclaiming that "nationalism is an essential component of religious faith," Hamas waited for the right moment to make a bid for community leadership.[12] Their opportunity arose during the buildup to the first Gulf war, when their most powerful rival, Arafat, made a strategic miscalculation. When one of the PLO's most important financiers, Iraq, attacked another, no less important backer, Kuwait, Arafat had to choose sides. By letting himself be photographed in a brotherly embrace with Saddam Hussein, the eventual loser in the conflict, Arafat forfeited the support of state and private financiers in the Gulf States, who thereafter funneled their money towards Hamas. Like Hezbollah in Lebanon, although without its professional level of organization, Hamas soon divided its functions between a political-civil arm and a military one, the Ezzedine al-Qassam Brigade.

The lion's share of Hamas's annual budget of $70 million or so[13] is spent on maintaining a network of hundreds of mosques, schools, orphanages, and wards that penetrates every village, refugee camp, and town in Gaza and the West Bank. Like Hezbollah in southern Lebanon, Hamas does much more than dispatch suicide bombers on missions; the movement also takes care of the families of suicide bombers, and concerns itself with the social welfare of its community as a whole. Hamas makes it possible for people to live—and to die. Financial support comes from the royal families and wealthy private individuals in the Gulf States, from the Palestinian diaspora, and even from Shi'ite Iran, and makes its way into the occupied territories mostly via Jordan.

Hamas's military wing, the Ezzedine al-Qassam Brigade, was named after the Syrian cleric who, with the help of Jerusalem's Grand Mufti Amin al Husseini, built up an armed organization in Haifa in the 1920s; this organization, called Black Hand, attacked the British Mandate troops until al-Qassam's violent death in 1935.[14] The Ezzedine al-Qassam Brigade started carrying out suicide attacks on Israeli soldiers as early as spring 1989, with the aim of turning Gaza into a living hell for Israel's occupying troops. The wording in the Hamas charter of 1988 was clear—"God is the goal, the Prophet the leader, and the Qur'an the constitution; the Holy War shows us the way, and our most heartfelt longing is to die for God"[15]—and the movement was banned by the Israeli government in September of the same year.[16]

After the dramatic abduction and murder of an Israeli soldier in December 1992, Israeli Prime Minister Yitzhak Rabin authorized the deportation to southern Lebanon of 415 leading cadres of Hamas and the smaller, strictly paramilitary Islamic Jihad. The exiles lived in tents in the southern Lebanese hills for a year, during which time sympathizers and members of Hezbollah took them under their wing and kept them supplied with food, blankets—and ideas. Up to that point, Palestinian Sunnis had had little contact with the Shi'ite resistance fighters in Lebanon; like their fellow Sunnis in the Gulf States, especially Saudi Arabia and Bahrain, they tended to view all Shi'ite minorities with suspicion as religiously unorthodox. Now, however, with plenty of time on their hands, and with the Israeli enemy in common, the exiled Palestinians came to know and rely on their Lebanese Shi'ite benefactors. Hezbollah seized the opportunity to initiate the Hamas leaders in both the techniques of suicide attacks and in its supposedly religious justification. And they were successful. In April 1993, the first year of the Oslo peace process and before the 415 exiles were allowed back home that December after endless diplomatic wrangling, the first "human bomb" rocked Israel. Hamas member Sahar Tamam Nabulsi, with a Qur'an next to him on the passenger seat of his white Mitsubishi, drove between two buses and blew himself up, killing another Palestinian and injuring eight Israelis.[17]

It is doubtful that the exchange of ideas and tactics during that southern Lebanese winter of 1992–93 was the sole reason Hamas turned to such tactics. Hamas leader Yahda Ayyash, the electrical engineering student who later came to be known as the legendary and notorious "Engineer," was recommending the use of human bombs in a letter written in 1990. "We paid a high price when we just used our slingshots and stones," observed Ayyash. "We must increase the pressure and the cost of the occupation in the form of human lives to such

an extent that it becomes intolerable." Martyrs, the only commodity
that the Palestinians possess in abundance, were to be the currency in
this battle. This tactic, he believed, would inflict the most painful
damage imaginable on the Israeli occupiers.[18]

What does Hamas stand for? It has never been entirely clear. At times
it resolutely refuses all compromise with the Jewish state, and claims
to work for its destruction. At other times, the call is not for an Islamic *Internationale,* but for a simple withdrawal on the part of the
occupiers. Hamas leader Sheik Yassin spoke in this latter vein in a
1997 interview: "I would like to make it clear that we're not fighting
the Jews because they're Jews, but because they attack and kill us, occupy our country, our houses, our children and our wives. They have
scattered us all over the place; a people with no home is what we are.
We want our rights. Nothing more. We love peace, but they hate it—
because people who rob others of their rights don't believe in peace.
Why shouldn't we fight? We have the right to defend ourselves."[19]

Hamas refuses to be pinned down, preferring to keep the greatest
possible number of options open.[20] Depending on the circumstances,
it wants peace and it wants to fight; it reveres the deaths of martyrs
but also claims to be prepared to negotiate a moratorium on the dispatch of martyr missions. As the Israeli Hamas experts, political scientists Shaul Mishal and Avraham Sela, argue, Hamas is less a
hermetic troop of fanatics than a complex, contradictory reflection of
the tensions and divisions of Palestinian society.[21]

In early 1994, an act of savagery committed by an Israeli gave Hamas
and all Palestinians skeptical of the peace process a crucial boost. An
American-born Israeli doctor, Baruch Goldstein, entered the Ibrahim
Mosque in Hebron with his Galil semiautomatic rifle and began shooting at the worshippers at prayer. The mosque was full that morning: it
was Ramadan, the holy month of fasting, and the 500 people present
seemed paralysed by the carnage that ensued—in the very place that
supposedly symbolized like nothing else the common ground existing

between the two Abrahamic religions. (Ibrahim is the Arabic equivalent of Abraham, whose grave is supposed to lie in a vault within the extended chambers shared by the seventh-century Ibrahim Mosque and a synagogue.) In all, twenty-nine worshippers were murdered and many others wounded before Goldstein was overwhelmed and murdered by the enraged crowd.

Palestinian and Israeli experts agree that this massacre was a key turning point. "Hamas interpreted it as a signal," claims Khalit Shikaki, "that the gloves were now off." Prime Minister Rabin's refusal to dismantle the Jewish settlement of Kiryat Arba, near Hebron, where Goldstein made his home, seemed to cast doubt on the seriousness of Israel's commitment to peace. The fact that Goldstein's grave soon became a place of pilgrimage for radical settlers and partisans of the notion of a Greater Israel rubbed salt into the wound.

This was the first serious setback for the hopes raised by the peace process. Khalil Shikaki, whose Ramallah-based Center for Policy and Survey Research had begun operation in the wake of the Oslo Accords, tracked the numbers in its opinion polls. In 1993, 65 percent of Palestinians in the occupied territories were in favor of Oslo, and 57 percent were prepared to amend the PLO's national charter and acknowledge formally Israel's right to exist. Economic expectations were similarly high: 65 percent expected peace to bring economic dividends. But this period of optimism was short lived. The Rabin government's continued expansion of the settlements, despite its agreement to withdraw—"land for peace" was the great motto of the day—followed by the Goldstein massacre, caused support for the peace process to drop to 51 percent.

These developments were not fatal to the prospects for peace, however. The Oslo process received a shot in the arm after Israel's occupying troops began withdrawing from broad swathes of the Gaza Strip and practically all the West Bank towns. After their withdrawal from Ramallah, Nablus, Tulkaram, Jenin, and Jericho, their occupation forces remained only in Hebron and East Jerusalem, and the majority of the Palestinian population could reasonably regard themselves as liberated. With each withdrawal, there was public jubilation and relief—and rapidly dwindling support for the radicals who were opposed to peace, both in the Islamist camp and in the PLO splinter groups. The handing over of the first towns gave an enormous boost to the PLO's prestige, and Arafat saw increasing approval for his strategic decision to treat Israel as a negotiation partner rather than as the enemy. Hamas's internal conflicts made it difficult for it to respond effectively in the mid-1990s. While its foreign leadership in Damascus and Amman continued to boycott all attempts at reconciliation, local leaders in Gaza and the West Bank were increasingly tempted to share in the new Palestinian power that had established itself under Arafat's aegis, and began discreetly distancing themselves from the leadership abroad. Ignoring Hamas's official boycott of Israeli-elections, at least ten prominent Hamas members registered themselves as independent candidates for local elections in 1995. And even the most radical Hamas cells stuck to the cease-fire they had negotiated with Arafat in Cairo, although they refused to acknowledge it officially in order to save face.[22] Things remained, by local standards, quiet.

Then, on January 5, 1996, an explosion in a house in Gaza killed Yahya Ayyash, the "Engineer," a leading strategist and bomb maker for Hamas. The Israeli authorities held Ayyash responsible for at least seven attacks causing seventy-six deaths and more than thirty injuries, and made no particular effort to disguise the involvement of their secret service, Mossad, in the carefully planned attack.

While the Israelis considered this a great strategic victory, and Minister for Security Moshe Shahal expressed his "relief,"[23] the assassination handicapped the Palestinian Authority in its internal struggle with the Islamist radicals. Given the scope of local outrage—some 200–300,000 people joined the ranks of the funeral procession—Arafat felt obliged to give a full hero's send-off to the very man who had previously been his most dangerous opponent. He declared the slain Hamas leader to be a "holy martyr," ordered a twenty-one-gun salute, and sent high-ranking leaders of an autonomous Palestine to the funeral. A Palestinian representative to the Knesset (the Israeli parliament), Asmi Bisara, explained the reasons for Ayyash's popularity: Ayyash "embodied all the hopes of the Palestinian youth. He was a have-not who came from an impoverished village and who received an education. Palestinians were inspired to see this young man from an impoverished background rise to become the greatest rival of Rabin and the Israeli security force. He was a role model for those who are accustomed to seeing themselves as victims. With his criminal activities, he gave them the feeling that they could fight back."[24]

The Israeli authorities felt that by blowing up the "Engineer"—his head was blown off by an exploding cell phone—they had both literally and symbolically decapitated an entire movement. Their message appeared to be: you can't escape from us. We're infinitely superior—and we build better bombs. But with its leader turned into a popular martyr, Hamas was goaded into retaliation. Barely two months after the January 1996 assassination, it sent a message of its own back to Israel. "*You* are the ones who are powerless against *our* weapons" was Hamas's response. "You can kill us, but, as you see, we remain unbowed. We are prepared to kill ourselves and will take you with us if we want—and where we want."[25]

On February 25, 1996, young suicide bombers bombed a bus on Route 18, killing themselves and twenty-six other people. The following day, outside Ashkelon, a driver raced his car into a crowd of people, killing a female passerby, before he was shot dead by bystanders. After months of calm, the country was in a daze. For a week, the country mourned the victims of these attacks. Cinemas, theatres, and even restaurants remained practically empty.[26] Then, despite the increased police presence, the horror repeated itself. As if to mock these security measures and Prime Minister Shimon Peres's pledge to wage "total war" against Hamas, Jerusalem's Bus Route 18 was targeted yet again. In a narrow part of Jaffa Street, a third suicide bomb exploded in the early morning of March 3, killing nine Israelis, two Palestinians, five Rumanian workers who had been brought into the country to replace Palestinian migrant labor, and two tourists.

The twenty-four-year-old attacker from Hebron had managed to get into Jerusalem despite heavy barricades around the Palestinian areas. The following day, a fourth attacker blew himself up in a Tel Aviv shopping mall. Twelve people died.

The attacks made Peres—who was in the midst of an election campaign against a resurgent, right-wing Likud Party led by Benjamin Netanyahu—look helpless, a paper tiger. "Three months to go," declared the graffiti at the scene of the attacks: three until the Israeli national elections that pitted Peres, who had been vaulted into the prime ministership after Rabin's assassination at the hands of a Jewish right-wing extremist in November 1995, against his challenger Netanyahu.[27] It only took a few days, in the course of which five suicide attacks blew sixty-nine people to pieces, to bring about a virtual national emergency, to stop the peace process, and to turn Shimon Peres into a loser-in-waiting. After the attacks, Peres's lead in the election polls melted away, and Netanyahu's support surged as he promised to shut the Palestinians off in autonomous cantons, guarded by Israeli troops.[28]

❖

When Netanyahu took over government, he promised security, and—as he pledged during one of his first cabinet meetings, as reported by the Israeli daily *Ha'aretz*—"liquidation" of the Hamas leaders. Soon, however, a botched assassination, aimed at eliminating one of the sources of terror, served instead to multiply these sources.

Netanyahu's debacle began in September 1996, when the Israeli secret service tracked down a Hamas leader, Khaled Meshal, in Amman, Jordan—the capital of the only Arab state other than Egypt with a formal peace treaty with Israel. It promptly dispatched two of its agents to Amman's Intercontinental Hotel, who, armed with counterfeit Canadian passports, checked in disguised as Canadian tourists. They began shadowing Meshal, and in the early morning of September 25, ambushed him in front of his office, sprayed something into his ear, and fled. Meshal's bodyguard gave chase and caught them with the help of a Jordanian policeman, who took the supposed tourists off with him to the nearest police station, whereupon their cover was blown in short order.[29]

While all this was going on, the poison injected into the Hamas leader's ear was taking effect. Meshal started vomiting; in the hospital, he couldn't breathe, and had to be put on a ventilator. He developed a high temperature, and responded to no medication, much to the bafflement of all the doctors. King Hussein, informed by the Jordanian secret service about what had transpired, angrily informed Netanyahu that he had the choice of either supplying an antidote or seeing his two agents tried and hanged.

In a gesture of contrition, half the Israeli cabinet, including Netanyahu himself, traveled to Amman. Ariel Sharon, then infrastructure minister, negotiated the release of the two agents in return for the release not only of several dozen Palestinian prisoners but also—and this was an especially bitter pill for the Likud government—of Hamas leader Sheikh Ahmed Yassin, who was granted permission to remain in Gaza. Yassin, who had been in prison since 1989, was released on October 1.[30]

Hamas could hardly have tailored a greater victory for themselves. Thousands gathered in Gaza. "We'll sacrifice our blood for Hamas!" roared the young people until they were hoarse.[31] Yassin's homecoming was staged like a rock concert. An hour before midnight, amid a general buzz of great expectation normally reserved for rock stars, an old man in a wheelchair appeared before a crowd of thousands. He was half deaf, crippled since his youth, his sight partially damaged, his falsetto voice barely audible—and for all that, at the very pinnacle of his power as Hamas's spiritual leader.

Henceforth, Hamas surged in the opinion polls and, over the next few years, drew level with Arafat's Fatah movement.[32] Arafat's cause was not helped by the fact that throughout all the peace negotiations under the framework of the Oslo Accords, whether the Israeli government was controlled by the Labor Party of Rabin, Peres, and Barak, or by the Likud of Netanyahu or Sharon, not a single Jewish settlement on the West Bank or in Gaza was cleared. Instead, new

ones sprang up, existing settlements expanded, and the number of settlers increased.

On March 27, 2001, Dia Tawil, a nineteen-year-old engineering student from Ramallah, blew himself to pieces at a bus stop in northern
Jerusalem when he detonated a nail bomb, injuring dozens.[33] Once
again, Israel's security forces sought the brains behind the bomber—
the string-puller or strategist—only to discover that such people are
hardly necessary anymore. Here was simply the case of a highly talented student of electrical engineering at the best university in the autonomous zone, who one day decided to blow himself to bits.

"I had other plans for my son," says Dia's father, Hussein Tawil,
who simply doesn't understand it, and searches for reasons. The family, he says from the depths of a plush couch, was active in the resistance to the occupation before the Oslo Accords, "but then, we
thought, well, everything will be okay," and he dedicated his energies
to his little shop and his life. But so far as his son was concerned, it
was the calm before the storm. The knick-knacks on the wall above
the sofa have been joined by several pictures of "Dia the Martyr." A
delegation from Hamas had turned up saying "mabruk!"—"congratulations!" No, he never chucked them out, says Hussein, kneading his
hands; that wouldn't have done, either. "But why? Why my son?"

And why, one might also ask, here in Ramallah, the West Bank's
wealthiest town, which the ghetto dwellers of Gaza refer to as if it
were Paris? A town which blossomed like no other, and whose total
number of inhabitants has rocketed to almost 100,000 since 1983? If
peace between the Israelis and Palestinians ever seemed possible, it
was here. There are no saints buried here; Jesus wasn't resurrected
here; and Mohammed didn't ride off into the sky from here. It's not a
place full of the fateful yearning for God like Jerusalem or Hebron; no
poverty-stricken camp like Gaza; but, rather, simply, the most prosperous town in the whole West Bank. When I first visited the town at

the end of 1995, Hani, the proprietor of Ramallah's first computer shop, proudly told me about Radio "Love and Peace," which had started broadcasting shortly before and which played jazz. We sat at Angelo's, Palestine's first pizzeria. Nobody at the time would ever have thought that, one day, suicide assassins would start out on their journey from Ramallah, too; or that schoolchildren would go into raptures about martyrs and spend their lunch breaks discussing what cakes they'd like to have at their funerals.

❋

The summer holidays are almost upon Palestine's schoolchildren when an entire class is made to stand before several foreigners, including me, and answer questions in a disciplined manner. No, they never go to the front line. No, definitely not. At recess, however, when they practice using their slingshots, they come up to us individually to say: "Of course we go!" The children, whom nobody sends and nobody stops, stand in the school yard and then discuss the last funeral of one of their schoolmates. "It's best if you die in the month of Ramadan, because that counts double for Paradise," one of them declares. A second fantasizes about the details of a great martyr's banquet after his self-sacrifice: at such a great celebration, he declares, there should be chocolate cakes with coconut flakes, his favorites. The headmaster overhears this, and comes over to me, intoning with an air of resignation, "We know it's a bad idea to run at heavily armed people with stones. But we can't stop it! As a living person here, you're nothing. As a dead person you can become a hero, at least for a moment"—the fifteen minutes of fame that Andy Warhol once predicted would be the lot of everyone. What will become of this young boy, who fantasizes about his post-mortem martyr banquet? The headmaster pauses. "I don't know. It doesn't make any difference to him anymore whether he's shot dead while throwing stones or blows himself up."

Israeli secret service analysts and their colleagues in social science research think tanks have spent years working on a profile of the "typical suicide assassin," only to conclude that there isn't one. Psychologist Ariel Merari of Tel Aviv University has painstakingly amassed dozens of biographies of suicide bombers, and presumably knows more about them than anyone else in Israel. Merari, who has been studying suicide in all its forms since the late 1970s, no longer sees any way to draw a narrow profile of today's would-be attacker. The more he looks into the biographies, the more the clichés crumble. External factors such as poverty or loneliness seem barely to play any role: the attackers come both from the poorest areas of Gaza and from Ramallah, the West Bank's wealthiest and most cosmopolitan town. "Today's suicide commandos," concludes Merari, "are a mirror image of their society." You find men from the lumpenproletariat along with university graduates, poor people, and also the sons of millionaires. They are still primarily—though not only—people of the faith. I asked if the attackers were more religious than their families, and it was so in only a third of cases." It was also wrong to assume, he said, that the attackers are picked by some organization without their knowledge, then programmed and sent off on their missions like booby-trapped automatons. "No group can just get someone to do that. At most, they can strengthen existing dispositions, but at the end of the day, it comes from the individual himself, from his experiences, from his beliefs." The original assumption—that the suicide bombers were exclusively isolated, young, poor, ultra-religious people with no prospects—might have applied in some degree to the first attackers. But nowadays "none of that is right anymore," admits Ephrahim Kam, a retired major of the Israeli military secret service who heads the Jaffe Center for Strategic Studies in Tel Aviv. "More and more, we see that the attackers are well-trained—just like the pilots who crashed their planes into the Twin Towers of the World Trade Center. And they don't strike you anymore as being particularly religious."[34]

In fact, it's precisely the well-educated, rather than the indigent, who take the lead in advocating violence, as Khalik Shikaki's opinion polls reveal. Shikaki confesses to having been surprised by these results. "It goes against trends in the rest of the world, but here the level of approval for violence rises in line with the level of education." It's not the mob, not the illiterate, who are goaded into violence, but precisely the well-educated, well-informed people who conclude that armed struggle is the only way out of the current situation.[35]

Why the upsurge in support for suicide attacks among educated Palestinians since the mid-1990s? Plucking a faded, well-thumbed paperback off an office shelf stuffed with scholarly literature on the roots of terrorism and suicide, Ariel Merari says he thinks he has part of the answer. The paperback, entitled *Why Men Rebel,* is a 1970 study of civil unrest among blacks in America by the sociologist Ted Gurr. "Black Americans," as Gurr argues, "didn't go to the barricades when things really were going badly for them, but at precisely the moment when their situation began to get better—when what they were getting wasn't in line with what they had been expecting. This is precisely the situation we have here: after Oslo, there was such a feeling of hope among the Palestinians that they would get their freedom, their state and, finally, their dignity. And at the start, there were concrete, tangible signs of progress: the cleared towns, the flags, the uniforms, that people could be proud of." But then pride waned; Arafat's Palestinian Authority proved to be corrupt and undemocratic; the Palestinian towns remained isolated islands, cut off from each other by Israeli security checkpoints, between which it was even more difficult to travel than before. Moreover, the building of Israeli settlements on land that Palestinians consider their own has continued unabated. Now it seems that they've lost all they had hoped for. "The only thing that counts for these youngsters, if you believe their last wills, is their battle, their courage, their power. They write about the Israeli occupation, about humiliation, and the Arab glory of the early days. About Muhammad, his companions, and their bravery. Ultimately, the vast majority of suicide bombers are quite normal people—but fearless, and with strong convictions."

It's the impotence that Eyad El-Sarraj, head of the Gaza Mental Health Project, refers to as the strongest driving force. "We're all powerless here, but some can bear it, while others can't. Personally, I believe that there are humans who can't bear to lose control over their destiny in this way. Taking your own life—and even your death—

literally into your own hands—along with the lives and deaths of perhaps two dozen others—is the ultimate power."

"Said" means "happy" in Arabic, and Said, a bricklayer's son, did indeed seem to have been a happy child. Old family photos show him
with friends on a boat trip; in the garden under the fig tree; riding a
camel with his father at the Dead Sea. This same father, in April 2001,
publicly declared that he was proud of the fact that his son just killed
himself and twenty-one other people. He had no regrets, he told a journalist from Abu Dhabi TV: "If I had twenty children, I'd send them all
off to Israel to blow themselves up and to kill some Israelis."[36]

"What was I supposed to say?" he asks plaintively weeks later, at
home in the small Jordanian town of Ruseifa. Should he have added to
his own pain by admitting that his son's death was senseless? "Mabruk,"
murmured those who entered his house as news of his son's deed made
its way round the neighborhood—congratulations on the honor of having become the father of a martyr. The family served lemonade, tea,
mocha, and confectionery—the same eerie ritual every time, set against
the backdrop of a photographic montage of the bomber-son. But just
weeks after the buffet reception, the father produces a photo album
filled with Said's pictures only reluctantly, and is just as hesitant to talk
about his son. He has fetched two neighbors to be by his side, to help
him maintain his composure. "I have to be proud of him!" When, despite a herculean effort at self-control, tears begin flowing after all, he
leaves the sparsely furnished living room, and one of the neighbors
picks up his thread: "Said died as a son of Palestine!"

Leyla Atschan, a psychologist from Ramallah, has heard it all before. She is driven to Nablus twice a week, where she counsels groups
of traumatized children and depressive women in the surrounding villages, including two mothers of suicide bombers. Atschan is blind, and
perhaps her handicap allows her to pick up subtle inflections in people's
voices that others miss. "They always talk about how proud they are,
yes, truly proud of their sons' actions—but it almost physically pains

me to hear how violently they have to keep their voices steady while they're talking, how they try to stop themselves from falling apart. I then try very carefully to give them back the legitimacy of grief. A mother is a mother, but of course everyone tries to act within the bounds of normality, for they give us a foothold. But nowadays the norms are horrific." Wherever you visit the families of the "human bombs," in Gaza, Nablus, Ramallah, or Hebron, you always find the same veneer of pride, the same platitudes. The more distant the friends and relatives are, the more proud they are. But beneath the bluster, there's a kind of silence; the parents either say nothing, or say, "What he did just has to have been right!"

Leyla Atschan, who still holds an American passport, returned to Palestine during the mid-1990s, when there was still lingering optimism in the air about the prospects for a lasting piece. Her decision to stay, and to sink her life savings into an apartment of her own in Ramallah, coincided with the gradual crumbling of the Oslo Accords. Now she is trapped in the cage that is Ramallah—one of 200 isolated enclaves of Palestinian territory, surrounded in every direction by Israeli roadblocks and checkpoints, where passage to other enclaves only several miles away is purchased with hours of waiting, intensive and arbitrary searches, and daily indignities and humiliations.

Israel refuses to negotiate about anything at all so long as Arafat or his successor hasn't put a stop to terrorism. But there's no prospect of any particular result that would make it worthwhile to enter into negotiations. Ariel Sharon isn't willing to discuss a halt to the expansion of Jewish settlements in the occupied territories and to the routine seizure of Palestinian lands, much less discuss the status of Jerusalem and a right of return for the Palestinian refugees of 1948. In any case, he's in no position to do so without risking his own position: the ultra-right-wing parties could terminate his governing coalition.

Sharon's policy is the iron fist and "targeted liquidations" of Hamas and Islamic Jihad leaders. But no sooner have the targeted real or supposed leaders been incinerated in their cars by rockets fired from Israeli helicopters, than Hamas and Islamic Jihad hit back with their undeniably effective countermeasures: people who are willing to sacrifice their lives.

In the early years of the Oslo process, Hamas and Islamic Jihad conducted suicide attacks not just in retaliation for Israeli army actions, but also simply to sabotage the peace process. But these were highly risky ventures for the two organizations, costing them popular support, and exposing them to persecution by Arafat's security services. The more recent attacks, committed for the most part in retaliation, are much more effective. They gratify the thirst for revenge, and find much stronger popular acceptance.

The ineffectiveness—the futility—of the Israeli government's policy of targeted liquidations has been apparent to the keenest Israeli observers of the situation for some time. As former Israeli intelligence head Ami Ayalon puts it, "We won't get rid of people's convictions by killing their leaders. So long as there is no political perspective, we just make things worse by so doing; we just create more suicide bombers."[37] Similarly, the Hebrew University political scientist Shlomo Avineri suggests that it was "totally nonsensical to believe that these killings could solve the Hamas problem."[38]

Despite all the barricades, despite all the retaliation measures, including the "preventive liquidations" and the demolition of the suicide bombers' family homes, nothing stops them. None of the groups who train, equip, and dispatch the volunteers ever appear to be weakened by the murder of one of their leaders.

With increasing numbers of Palestinians of all ages and backgrounds declaring themselves ready to embark on a fatal mission with a belt of bombs strapped to their waists, the time needed to recruit and train them for missions has dropped dramatically since the mid-1990s. According to Eyad El-Sarras of the Gaza Mental Health Project, candidates formerly "had to spend forty-eight hours under the earth, in a grave, next to a corpse. If they managed that, then the training began: they learnt how the bombs operate, how to completely isolate themselves from their friends and relatives in order to prevent them from bailing out—or from being discovered." Nowadays, however, wider social acceptance of the practice makes all this unnecessary. Neither do the most recent volunteers require drugs, as many have assumed. Yehuda Hiss, a specialist in forensic medicine, who has examined the remains of many attackers, has yet to find any trace of drugs: "They are motivated by some psychological motive prior to their attack. They are fully lucid at the moment of death."[39]

No sinister Pied Pipers need to dance through the streets, enticing emotionally unstable youths into indoctrination camps and turning them into unthinking robots. The young volunteers are not forced, and are instead interrogated and scrutinized in order to select those most likely to perform efficiently, as a Hamas cadre delights in reporting: "The selection process is complicated by so many people wanting to be taken on this journey of honor! If we choose one, countless others are disappointed. They have to learn to be patient and to wait until God calls them!"[40] Hamas's biggest problem, says this cadre, almost regretfully, "are the hordes of young men who come banging on our door, begging us to send them on a mission. It's difficult to choose just a few of them. The ones we send away just keep coming back, badgering us, begging us, beseeching us to accept them for a mission!"

And yet a strong majority of Israel's Jewish population continue to support Sharon's course up to now. He was re-elected as Israel's prime minister at the start of 2002, despite the fact that neither the "targeted liquidations" nor the reoccupation of almost all the West Bank territory ceded in the 1990s, have stemmed the violence. Indeed, nothing appears likely to break the intensifying, dreary cycle of retaliation in the near future. The desperation is growing, as is the hatred on both sides. The dry, awful sounds of detonations, and the subsequent ambulance sirens and howls of pain, seem fated to continue. As Amos Oz wrote in 1967, at a different political juncture: "The heroes of the tragedy, who are devouring each other in the name of justice and purity, are destroying and annihilating one another through the sheer force of logical consequences."[41]

Suicide or Martyrdom?

MODERN ISLAM AND THE FEUD OF THE FATWAS

❋

The Qur'an is but ink and paper, and it does not speak for itself.
Instead, it is human beings who give effect to it according to their
limited personal judgments and opinions.
—Imam Ali, son-in-law of the Prophet Muhammad and fourth caliph

He who wants to kill himself because he's sick of being
alive—that's suicide. But if someone wants to sacrifice his soul
in order to defeat the enemy and for God's
sake—well, then he's a martyr.
—Abdelaziz al-Rantisi, second-in-command of the political
wing of Hamas in Gaza

Traditionally, when Muslims in predominantly Islamic countries wanted guidance from their religious authorities, they went to the mosque on Friday and listened to the local cleric's sermon. Nowadays, by contrast, in Gaza as in Jerusalem, Beirut, Cairo, Riyadh, and Dubai, Muslims gathering together at Friday worship in mosques throughout the region are more likely to hang on every word of one and the same man who tells them what's right and what's wrong, what's *halal* ("allowed") and what's *haram* ("forbidden"). That man is Sheikh Yusuf al-Qaradwi, perhaps the most popular Sunni theologian of the Arab world. His popularity is due neither to his training at Cairo's prestigious Al-Azhar University, nor to his venerable age, nor to his pedigree (he comes from a notable family)—but rather to his media profile. Qaradwi has his own highly rated TV show on the region's most popular satellite channel, Al-Jazeera, based in Qatar.

Every week, Qaradwi interprets the world in "*Shari'a* (Islamic law) and life." Anyone who hears him quickly grasps that the religious justification for political actions has a great deal to do with political judgment. And Qaradwi is a very active commentator on contemporary politics, passing judgment on political actors, in the Islamic world and abroad, all the time. Of all the high-ranking Islamic theologians who condemned the attacks of September 11, Qaradwi was one of the quickest off the mark. "Our hearts bleed . . . despite our rejection of the U.S. policies towards Israel," he stated on September 12, 2001, of the previous day's events. "Even in times of war, Muslims are forbidden to kill civilians indiscriminately. This is a loathsome crime."[1] No, he continued, the attacks on the World Trade Center were definitely not "martyr operations," and the perpetrators would not enter Paradise. However, the "human bombs" dispatched by Hamas and Islamic Jihad on murderous missions in Israel were indeed performing acts of martyrdom pleasing to God, even if they hit women and children. For they are at war there. No, the bombing of Afghanistan by the United States wasn't, in his opinion, justified. Yes, Muslim soldiers in the U.S. forces must obey their orders—but, as Qaradwi pronounced one month later, "America meets terrorism with similar terrorism."[2] Qaradwi wants to be all things to all men in order to preserve his growing audience of millions, from Marrakesh to Muscat: an authority for the radicals in the Arab world, but also for moderate Arab rulers, and for Muslims in the diaspora, in Europe and the United States. His theological slalom course reflects the deep divisions within his community.

Western observers commonly assume that the Qur'an and tales handed down from the Prophet Muhammad contain unambiguous guidelines for what Muslims should and should not do. But that is a mistake. For over a millennium, Islamic legal authorities, claiming a basis for their edicts and other writings on divine authority, have created an ever-expanding body of jurisprudence; some of it is contradictory, some evinces quite daring interpretations—and all of it is available to support every conceivable argument. In this maze of interpretations, nothing is self-evidently certain. Whatever else it is, Islam is a belief system filled with infinite possibilities that can legitimate a wide range of practices as and when the need arises. Suicide bombing is one such practice—although its embrace is by no means shared by all—or even by the majority—of Muslims.

Suicide bombing is not an exclusively Islamic phenomenon. But even if secular civil war combatants like the Kurdish PKK and the Tamil Tigers have resorted to this powerful tactic of war, most of the suicide attacks of the last twenty years have occurred in predominantly Islamic countries and have been fed from the very depths of the Islamic tradition. The drivers of the exploding trucks that killed hundreds of American marines in Beirut in 1983 were Muslims; so are the more recent Palestinian "human detonators."

The notion of martyrdom arises and is nurtured by a combination of Qur'anic teachings, fatwas (religious rulings), and promises of Paradise from the Islamic tradition. As the medieval Sunni theologian Al-Bukhari describes it, God awaits the martyr with heavenly rewards: "The wounds of he who is injured while standing up for God's cause— and God knows exactly who is injured in this capacity—will have the scent of musk on the Day of Judgment. . . . Nobody in Paradise would wish to return to earth, with the exception of the martyr, who died in battle for God's cause. He would return to earth to be killed again ten times over after all the salutes accorded to him in Paradise."[3]

Who, in the Islamic tradition, can be called a martyr? The young war volunteers in Iran of the mid-1980s, who willingly threw themselves into Iraqi machine-gun fire and minefields? The driver of a pickup truck packed with explosives who plows into a military compound filled with sleeping soldiers? The young man who blows himself up with five kilos of TNT on a bus crammed with schoolchildren and seniors? To outsiders, it may seem like scholastic hair-splitting to ask whether someone who embraces certain death by dashing openly into enemy fire is a soldier falling in combat like any other, or a self-executioner, but according to the Islamic code of conduct there's a crucial difference between them. For few things have been a greater taboo in Islam than suicide. As honorable as it is to die in battle—that is, to die at someone else's hands in a worthy cause—so has it been considered shameful to wilfully take one's own life. The religious authorities of traditional Islam, like those of the other Abrahamic faiths, Judaism and Christianity, condemn those who commit suicide for ignoring the authority of God.

The ban on suicide has never been in place at all times and in all places. In late antiquity, self-imposed martyrdom was not yet detrimental to the individual's posthumous reputation, as the biographies of Seneca, Socrates, Cleopatra, and Marcus Antonius attest. In the Bible, too, there is no explicit injunction against suicide. The ban on suicide appeared in Christian Europe once Christianity began to attain political power. Augustine, an innovator across the board, initiated the move, which was followed by other early Church Fathers.

In Islam we find a similar pattern. There is no crystal-clear ban on suicide in the Qur'an,[4] although many interpreters and translators have attempted to read such a ban into an ambiguous verse. Much of the controversy stems from the meaning of a personal pronoun in surah 29 of part 5 of the Qur'an, *anfusakum*. It can mean both "you yourself" and "people like you," and the entire verse in which it appears[5] has been translated in all sorts of totally different ways: "Don't kill yourself either! For God is merciful"[6]; "Don't become a suicide . . ."[7]; ". . . and do not kill each other"[8]; "and do not commit suicide"[9]; and finally "don't kill those who share your own faith! . . ."[10]

The famous Qur'anic commentator and historian at-Tabari (858–923) offered an interpretation of the verse in question 1,100 years ago that remains highly influential today: "Don't kill your own kind!" In so far as all Muslims are followers of the same faith, reasoned at-Tabari, they can be regarded as tantamount to being a single individual. So if a Muslim kills another Muslim, it's as if he's killing himself. This interpretation seems plausible, as the rest of the verse, which concerns the rules for business dealings between Muslims, suggests something similar: "Do not deprive yourselves of your own wealth by cheating one another."[11]

By the ninth century, after the wave of Muslim conquests had given rise to a world empire under the banner of the Prophet, a ban on suicide was well-established in Islamic countries, with the promise of banishment to hell as punishment. Death brought about by one's own hand is unambiguously condemned in the works of those who hand down the Prophet's dictums, the *hadiths*. Only al-Bukhari dedicates an entire chapter to the topic: "On one occasion, the Prophet was present when a wounded man committed suicide. Consequently God himself said: 'My servant took his life into his own hands and thus pre-empted my decision. Therefore his entry into paradise is barred.'" In two further hadiths it says: "The Prophet said: he who throws himself off a mountain and commits suicide will burn in the fires of hell. He will stay there for all eternity and will eternally repeat his deed. He who poisons himself and commits suicide will poison himself with the poison in his hand for all eternity in the fires of hell. He who commits suicide with a sharp object will repeatedly cut his stomach open for all eternity in the fires of hell."[12] Even respectable deeds can't compensate for the sin of suicide. A tradition ascribed to the Prophet Muhammad names suicide in the same breath as other serious, unforgivable crimes.[13] A Muslim who commits suicide destroys God's creation and is to be punished accordingly. In the early eighteenth century, a fatwa pronounced suicide to be a greater crime than murder,[14] and at the start of the twentieth century, the condemnation of suicide took a turn which may seem grotesque to us today: it was viewed as an import from Europe, as an "immoral stance and a custom that is to be condemned; it is a punishment inflicted on us by Western civilizations. The idea of suicide is truly an inclination of the devil, thus there's no forgiveness for the man who commits it," wrote the Egyptian al-Manfaluti.[15]

Over the centuries, the stance in Christian Europe was hardly different. In the eyes of many practicing Christians today, suicide is regarded as sacrilege, as a sin and an act of rebellion against God's will. The only difference is that the influence of religious faith on everyday life has diminished rapidly in the Europe of the modern era, although England didn't abolish a law putting suicide on a par with murder until 1961.[16]

A time-honored taboo concerning suicide is also well established in Islam. Just as assuredly as the *shahid*, the martyr who dies in battle, is said to find a place at God's side in Paradise, so will the suicide find a place in hell. These two categories—the suicide and the martyr—have been at the heart of a theologians' dispute that has been carried on with ever-increasing urgency since 1983. What some have perceived as a straightforward and understandable intensification of martyrdom, others see as a transgression of authoritative boundaries drawn more than one thousand years ago.

In the post-revolutionary Iran of Ayatollah Khomeini, there was no theological controversy. Khomeini, whose word was law, saw the thousands of young war volunteers who detonated mines with their own bodies during the Iran-Iraq War as soldiers who had fallen in battle. In southern Lebanon of the early 1980s, by contrast, it required more interpretive dexterity to justify, in Islamic terms, the actions of Hezbollah's lethal drivers, who killed themselves along with hundreds of Americans, French, and Lebanese—soldiers and civilians alike.

Especially difficult for any ostensibly Islamic-inspired suicide bombing outfit to confront is a provision (*hukm*) of Islamic law that seems to forbid the martyr from putting his affairs in order before his death.[17] A farewell letter written beforehand, or a will, would (according to traditional Islamic legal scholars) make an act of martyrdom look like a premeditated suicide. Hezbollah is rather vulnerable on this front. To this day, every suicide bombing mission in which they are implicated features a prerecorded video testament in which the attacker clearly announces what he's about to do and give reasons for it, against the by now familiar backdrop of the Qur'an, Kalashnikovs, and the yellow Hezbollah flags. Likewise, those whose testimonies are written in advance and published in the "Princes of Paradise" column of the Hezbollah monthly newspaper *Baqiyat Allah* appear, strictly speaking, to have jeopardized their martyr status.

The most highly regarded and influential Shi'ite cleric outside Iran, Sheikh Hussein Fadlallah, had considerable difficulty finding a principled Islamic rationale for giving his blessing to Hezbollah's new weapon. Fadlallah who sets great store by his independence but still represents the highest religious authority for most Hezbollah members, was initially quite cool towards the attackers and their enablers. He warned them against using this last resort measure too often—whereupon the Hezbollah leadership went over his head and appealed to Teheran for a blessing for their "martyr operations." They got what they wanted, for at the time Ayatollah Khomeini was more inclined than Fadlallah to approve of Hezbollah's doings.[18] Fadlallah subsequently issued a fatwa declaring suicide attacks (referred to, interestingly enough, as explosions) legitimate, provided that the greatest possible number of enemies would be killed by them; this fatwa now had a whiff of expediency about it.[19]

The religious traditions of Palestinian Muslims pose other challenges, and in fact are less predisposed towards the reverence of martyrs and saints than the Shi'ite tradition in Lebanon. Theirs is a conservative, rationalist type of Islam with no place for spiritualized folk belief in local saints, no mysticism, and no tolerance for Sufis who dance themselves into ecstasy, as one can readily witness in Morocco, Libya, Egypt, and Pakistan. Although the Islam of the Palestinians has become stricter over the years—especially in Gaza, the stronghold of the Islamists—religion in Palestine is still shaped by the political situation. All Palestinian religious movements define their actions in terms of the nation's political struggle. Although the word "Islamic" does indeed appear in Hamas's Arabic acronym, it is as an adjective, not a noun. The noun is "defense"—of the nation.

From its beginnings, the PLO was a secular nationalist organization. Arafat's role model was Egypt's charismatic leader Gamal Abdel-Nasser, not the ideologues of the Muslim fraternity. In the course of time, however, the Palestinian side began to mirror the arguments of the messianic Zionists on the Israeli side, who defended their claim to the land by invoking promises of God and the Hebrew

Bible that were presented as so clear cut, they might as well have been officially recorded in the Office of Land Registry. Palestinians began wheeling God out in turn, developing myths of jihad that could be mobilized against "the Jews," who had occupied the holy land "of the Muslims," and the rest of the Islamic world encouraged this trend. In 1989, for example, during the first Palestinian intifada, the arch-conservative grand mufti of Saudi Arabia, Sheikh Abdulaziz bin Baz, issued a fatwa declaring the Palestinians' opposition to be a jihad and, as such, a battle implicating all Muslims, and one that all Muslims should accordingly take part in.

This groundwork led to the 1995 televised declaration of Yusuf al-Qaradawi, Al-Jazeera's celebrity TV cleric, that Palestinian suicide attacks are justified. "These operations," intoned Qaradawi, "are the highest form of jihad and are most certainly permitted by the Shari'a, which says, after all: spread fear among your enemies and those of God!"[20] Qaradawi had to make his own, carefully wrought distinction between suicide and martyrdom. "A person who commits suicide kills himself for his own benefit. But a person who becomes a martyr sacrifices himself for the faith and the nation. Whereas a person who kills himself has given up all hope in himself and in God, the mujahid, the warrior, has total faith in God's mercy. He does battle with the enemy and the enemy of God with this new weapon which Providence has put in the hands of the weak so that they are in a position to fight the powerful and arrogant. The mujahid becomes a living bomb who decides when and where the explosion will take place in the enemy's midst; who renders them helpless in the face of the brave martyr who has sold his soul to Allah, and who has sought out martyrdom for God's sake."[21] In these operations, insisted Qaradawi, even women and children aren't to be spared, "for Israel is in its very essence a military society. Both men and women serve in the army. To be sure, if a child or an old person is killed in the process, then it's not intentional but an oversight; a mistake for reasons of military necessity. Necessity justifies what is forbidden."

Here we have a case of a fatwa driven by the political convictions of the issuer, and not just any issuer: Qaradawi's authority comes not from his years of Islamic legal study, but from the celebrity of a highly rated television program.

❈

The political struggles that underlie recent supposedly religious debates within Islam over suicide attacks were revealed with striking clarity in the feud of the fatwas that began in April 2001. Saudi Grand Mufti Sheikh Abdulaziz bin-Abdullah al-Ashaikh began the skirmish by issuing a clear rejection of terrorist attacks against civilians, declaring that "the Shari'a provided no justification" either for "so-called suicide attacks" or for aircraft hijackings. "Such attacks," he declared, "are not part of the jihad, and I fear that they are just suicides plain and simple. Although the Qur'an permits, indeed demands, that the enemy be killed, this has to happen in such a way that it doesn't run contrary to the religious laws."[22]

The Grand Mufti's remarks, while not a fatwa in a formal legal sense, could not be taken lying down by those in the Islamic world with a strong vested interest in these attacks and their propagation. Palestinian clerics and politicians immediately responded with counter-fatwas: the mufti of Jericho, Sheikh Muhammad Ismail al-Jamal, published a fatwa which for the first time clarified the "huge difference" between "martyrdom, which is both permitted and desirable in Islam, and suicide, which leads straight to hell."[23] Hamas Sheikh Hamid al-Bitawi put forward the thesis that "if infidels occupy even the tiniest bit of Muslim land, as happened when the Jews occupied Palestine, the jihad becomes a duty for every individual," and thus suicide attacks become permissible.[24] Dr. Abdulaziz al-Rantisi, second in command of Hamas's political wing, finally explained that it was all a question of definition: "If a martyr wants to kill himself because he's sick of being alive, that's suicide. But if he wants to sacrifice his soul in order to defeat the enemy and for God's sake—well, then he's a martyr."[25]

Opponents to the Saudi grand mufti's attack on the legitimacy of suicide bombing practice did not shy away from playing political hardball. Opposition newspapers based in London immediately started writing about the "American fatwa" that could only have arisen because of pressure from the United States and the Saudi royal family.[26] Abdulaziz al-Ashaikh's credibility as an interpreter of Islamic law was also called into question, something that would never have happened with his esteemed predecessor as grand mufti, the legendary Abdulaziz bin Baz.

The target of the so-called "American fatwa" of al-Ashaikh was less likely the Palestinians than Osama bin Laden and his followers. A Saudi diplomat and one of his Western counterparts claim that al-Ashaikh's proclamation originated in a vigorous attempt of the Saudi royal family to prevent further al-Qaeda suicide attacks. One month before the proclamation, in March 2001, a planned attack was foiled by Saudi authorities, who subsequently took dozens of suspects into custody and called influential sheikhs in for stern warnings. Apparently the authorities then called upon Grand Mufti al-Ashaikh to cover their backs theologically—to issue a fatwa-like statement classifying suicide attacks as precisely that: suicide, not martyrdom.[27]

Saudi Arabia is not the only Arab state in which the government leans on religious authorities to issue the "right" Islamic edicts. Sheikh Muhammad Said Tantawi, grand mufti at Cairo's Al-Azhar University and one of the highest authorities in Sunni Islam, was also apparently told by Egyptian president Hosni Mubarak to provide a ruling along the same lines. Tantawi, concerned with maintaining favor with Egypt's autocratic leadership, but also keen to keep his options open, issued a cleverly worded declaration in April 2001 that was both supportive of and opposed to suicide attacks. "Suicide operations," he stated, "are an act of self-defense and a type of martyrdom so long as their intention consists of killing the enemy's soldiers, but not women and children."[28] This statement of qualified support for suicide attacks in fact represented a shift away from a much harsher condemnation of them issued in August 1998, in the wake of attacks on U.S. embassies in Kenya and Tanzania. At that time, he condemned "any explosion which leads to the deaths of innocent women and children. That is a crime committed only by traitors and cowards, for a man who has even the slightest trace of respect would never carry out such acts!"[29] And yet in May 1998, the ever-flexible Tantawi had asserted precisely the opposite: "It is the right of all Muslims, Palestinians, and Arabs to blow themselves up in the heart of Israel. A noble death is better than a life of humiliation. There is no other way than the battle, the jihad, and whosoever tries to evade it, is not a believer!"[30]

The confusion is real. Egyptian lawyer Taufiq ash-Schawi, who made Tantawi's equivocal April 2001 fatwa public, tried to argue that there was some logical coherence underlying all this. Fatwas issued against suicide attacks, he asserted, refer only to peacetime actions, whereas more supportive but equally valid fatwas apply in times of war.[31] This double standard—wholly unprecedented in the Islamic tradition before recent times—was defended at two conferences of Islamic jurists in January 2002 in Qatar's capital Doha, and in June 2002 in Teheran. Conference attendees agreed that suicide attacks are permitted in Israel as part of the struggle against the Jewish state's military policy of occupation, but forbidden elsewhere.[32] The only dissenting voice at the Doha conference, the Saudi Sharia professor Hassan Ibn Mohammed Safar, insisted, against the consensus, that suicide attacks represented a squandering of human life and the blind killing of innocents, and provoked general hatred against the Muslims.[33]

This is simply politics, the kind of politics that attempts to give practical decisions and popular opinions some kind of retroactive Islamic legal basis, even if a wholly fabricated one. If a given fatwa does not conveniently support one's political orientation or policy, its originator is forthrightly and passionately denounced as an ignoramus or a traitor. "Fatwas that were issued against these heroes don't originate from religious authorities," declared a Gaza-based Islamist newspaper heatedly, "but from a group to whom the Sharia is completely alien. They are presumably serving their regime, or are police agents."[34]

How one deals with suicide attacks depends greatly on what motives are presumed to lie behind them. If one believes them to be a result of political desperation, a political response is called for. If, alternatively, they are thought to spring from the perversity of individuals, who for their own lascivious reasons are determined to get into paradise in order to have sexual relations with virgins, and who are impervious to reason—then it would be appropriate to deal with them as if they were a criminal sect; to arrest them, isolate them, fight them.

In Israel and in the United States, the supposedly sexual motives of young male suicide bombers have been the object of serious media attention since 2001. When the American TV network CBS broadcast a report on *60 Minutes* on August 19, 2001, about Hamas, it included the translation of an interview between an American journalist and the Hamas functionary Muhammad Abu Wardeh, whose description of how he had recruited a candidate for suicide attacks was translated thus: "I described to him how God compensates the martyr for sacrificing his life for his country. If you become a martyr, God will give you seventy virgins, seventy married women and joy for all eternity." But after the first broadcast of the interview, Muslim centers in the United States from California to Washington complained that the translation was faulty to the point of being entirely fabricated. The entire tape was played once again in the presence of two experienced and well-qualified translators. Also present was Hafiz al-Mirazi Osman, the head of Al-Jazeera's Washington office. All three heard a quite different message in the key passage of the original: "There are many things in paradise. Tradition says that everything the new arrival wishes for is at hand. That includes seventy-two angels . . . or women."

At issue was the correct meaning of the small Arabic word *huri*, which appeared in the interview in the plural form, *hur'ain*. Osman and one of the translators, Dr. Mather Hathout of the Islamic Center of Southern California in Los Angeles, insisted that it meant "angel" or "heavenly being," and had no gender connotations nor anything remotely to do with sex. CBS insisted that it concerned "virgins," that Hamas was promulgating sexually charged pictures of paradise in order to entice gullible, sex-starved young Palestinian men into self-sacrifice. Translator Hathout begged to differ: "There is nothing in the Qur'an or in Islamic teachings about seventy virgins or sex in paradise. It is ridiculous, and every true Muslim knows that!"[35]

An examination of Islamic interpretations of Qur'anic descriptions of paradise certainly reveals something other than lascivious desire, although those who insisted after the CBS controversy that the *huris* have always been gender-neutral, and that paradise, as depicted in the Qur'an and by the prophets, has nothing sensual about it, are on shaky ground.

In the Qur'an itself, the trappings of Paradise are very sketchily described: "dark-eyed" *huris* are waiting for the (male) believers, like "rubies and pearls"[36] in their value, color, and purity. Commentators over the centuries have painted Paradise in the most resplendent colors. In Paradise, "every man" is initially given "a palace in which there are seventy further palaces, every one of them decked out with seventy rooms made of hollow pearls. . . . Inside every room is a divan, richly decorated with garlands of pearls and hyacinths, . . . and every divan is covered with seventy rugs, all in various colors."[37] There, virgins await the men with "big black eyes" and "heaving breasts," "as if they were hyacinths and corals," and radiate an entire bouquet of scents: "saffron from their toes to their knees; musk from their knees to their breasts; ambergris from their breasts to their necks; and camphor from their necks to the top of their heads."[38] Some medieval depictions of Paradise are so fantastic that one ninth-century commentator dismissed them as nothing more than "a toy for little children."[39] Women in Paradise, according to one florid description, "are so beautiful that he will be able to see the very marrow of their bones through the flesh on their legs."[40] Yet another provides them with a rather unconventional beauty: women in Paradise "have neither buttocks nor anus, created as they were for the elimination of faeces—and there's nothing of that sort in paradise."[41] This suggests that while depictions of the sexual prowess of the male "Chosen Ones" in Paradise abound in these stories,[42] the sexual relations so described might well be meant metaphorically.

All debates about the sensual nature of Islamic depictions of paradise aside, there is still one serious problem with the assumptions of the aforementioned CBS report: the farewell letters of the typical suicide assassin these days rarely make mention of any of these sensuous visions. Rather, they typically express support for the political struggle, and the desire to see other martyrs. It is possible, of course, that some of these young men secretly fortify themselves for their immanent sacrifice with pornographic fantasies of an imagined eternal life to come, but stress more selfless, noble themes in their posthumously broadcast declarations. But an examination of many such testaments suggests that it is highly unlikely that sex, even the promise of never-ending sex with many women, is the main reason for their actions. The idea that yet another seventeen- or eighteen-year-old Palestinian, sexually frustrated and with no girlfriend, decided to swap misery for an orgy with one press of a button, does, however, make a good tabloid newspaper story.

Paradise, the promise of the continuation of existence, does play a role in most decisions to become a human bomb, but it serves as consolation much more than motive or cause. Belief in paradise, moreover, is a convenient mental device for contravening the suicide taboo. The prospect of paradise means that the attacker doesn't really take his own life, nor does he *want* to do so; he simply lives on, but in another place. This is the reasoning behind Gaza-based Islamic Jihad militant Ahmed Shamni's insistence in an interview with a journalist, that "if you want to be a holy martyr, you have to want to live!"[43] This is also why the death of a suicide assassin is not officially mourned but instead turned into its macabre opposite: a marriage celebration. Here, as an example, is a spring 2001 announcement of the death of an assassin, published in *Al-Istiqlal,* the irregularly appearing house organ of Islamic Jihad: "It is with great pride that we announce that the Palestinian Islamic Jihad is joining in matrimony the member of its military wing, martyr and hero Yasser al-Adhami with 'the dark-eyed ones.'"[44] And when Izzedin al-Masri blew himself up in front of a Sbarro Pizzeria in Jerusalem on August 9, 2001, killing fifteen guests and passersby, including several children, the Hamas functionary Ashraf Swaftah described the matrimonial-like ceremony held in al-Masri's honor: "His relatives distributed sweets and accepted their son as a bridegroom married to 'the black-eyed,' not as someone who had been killed and was being laid in the ground."[45]

But what *do* you get in paradise? Angels or Eros? Sexual playmates or a divine aura? In response to an Egyptian journalist's question, "Do people really have sex in paradise?" Sheikh Muhammad Said Tantawi, grand mufti at Cairo's Al-Azhar University, responded with an answer worthy of Solomon: "Only God knows that. He alone is privy to such private matters. For us, however, it's quite sufficient to know what the Qur'an says: it [Paradise] holds in readiness everything to gratify the soul and gladden the eye, and in it, you have life everlasting."[46]

Bushido Replaces *Allahu akbar*

THE JAPANESE KAMIKAZE

They hoped neither for reward, nor for Paradise.
In the end they didn't even hope for victory. The more
their comrades' death toll increased, the greater the
determination of those who remained to follow their
example, ashamed as they were of their attachment to life.
—Maurice Pinguet, French Japanologist

Actually they are still too young to drink alcohol.
—a Japanese commander on his fourteen- and fifteen-year-old
kamikaze pilots

The last lines that Uehara Ryoji wrote to his parents before embarking on May 11, 1945, on his final, one-way flight read as if the military leadership of Japan had been guiding his hand: "I regard it as the ultimate honor to have been selected for the special military unit that can be considered the most distinguished fighting unit of our noble fatherland."[1] He was not afraid of death, he insisted, but instead "replete with happiness for I am quite certain that I will meet my brother Tatsu once again. My last wish is that we may see each other again in heaven."

But a different picture emerges from other sections of this letter, jotted down by Uehara Ryoji on the evening before his aerial assault on

American warships near Okinawa. His words demonstrate just how clearly he saw through the role allotted to him in the murderous denouement of the final months of the war, and how unmoved he was by the rosy romanticism of heroic self-sacrifice on the battlefield. "As Special Unit pilots we turn into machines once we board our airplanes. We become molecules in a magnet drawn inexorably towards the enemy aircraft-carrier—devoid of personality, of emotions, and, of course, of reason. We become a machine whose function is to manipulate the control-column." It was quite clear to the 22-year-old, who prior to his military service had studied economics at Keio University in Tokyo, that "it cannot really be explained" in rational terms. It was not suicide, as the enemy supposed, but simply the military deployment of a machine that happened to be a human being—something that was possible only within the worldview of the Japanese. The final wish he addressed to his compatriots was that they would "turn our beloved Japan into a great and mighty empire."

Thus the farewell lines of a kamikaze pilot. Uehara Ryoji was one of over 2,000 pilots who departed on one-way missions between October 25, 1944, and August 15, 1945, the day of Japan's surrender.[2] Their task: to crash their bomb-laden aircraft on one of the U.S. ships that were inflicting serial losses on the Japanese in the Pacific and seemed to be advancing unstoppably on the Japanese heartland.

After their conquest of the Philippines at the beginning of 1942, the Japanese armed forces had not won a single important battle. Instead, one Pacific island after another had fallen into the hands of the Americans. Had Japan's rulers been concerned with preventing heavy losses, and in particular heavy sacrifices among the civilian population, the country would have surrendered long before August 1945. But capitulation was not an option in imperial Japan. Surrender to the "decadent West" was not to be countenanced.

In early October 1944, Vice Admiral Takijiro Onishi took up his new post as commander of the Philippines. He was convinced that the Japanese could be saved from outright defeat only by an entirely new strategy that transcended the bounds of standard military practice: "The salvation of our country lies in the hands of God's soldiers. The only way to destroy our opponent's fleet and thus get back on the road to victory is for our young men to sacrifice their lives by crashing their aircraft on enemy ships."[3] He was in no doubt whatever that they would be ready and willing to make such sacrifice: "What greater honor could there be for a warrior than to give his life for emperor and country?"[4]

The intention of the Japanese was to seriously weaken U.S. morale by demonstrating that they were determined to go to the most extreme lengths to prevail in the struggle, and that they were unwilling to surrender no matter what the cost. This strategy of terror worked in the initial stages. On October 25, 1944, brutally and without any warning, the first kamikazes came crashing down from the heavens on the Americans. Bill Simons, an aviation mechanic on the U.S. carrier *Santee,* cruising in the Leyte Gulf off the Philippine coast, at first thought the attack had happened by mistake: "We thought the pilot of the plane hadn't been able to pull her up in time."[5] But when a second plane came crashing down very soon afterwards, this time on the *Santee*'s sister ship, it dawned on him that it was no mistake, and that it also wasn't the doing of a single individual. "I reckon there's nothing else the Japs could have done that would have shaken the morale of U.S. troops more thoroughly than this did."

The American troops may have been completely thunderstruck by the kamikaze phenomenon, but decades before Admiral Onishi, the Japanese Imperial Army had already begun compensating for equipment shortages and inferior weaponry by encouraging suicidal attacks. In the Russo-Japanese War, for instance, swordfighters were used to attack machine-gun placements, despite the enormous losses that this entailed. This was a strategy born of sheer desperation, and one that could emerge only in an environment in which defeat was widely seen as the worst imaginable humiliation. Beyond all hope of victory, this option made it possible to die a glorious death and hence save face. Choosing life and therewith disgrace was simply not an option for the majority of kamikaze pilots.

In military parlance the suicide pilots were euphemistically termed *tokkotai*—an abbreviated form of *Tokubetsu kogekitai* or "Special

Attack Groups." The suicide pilots may not have altered the course of the war, but the fear engendered by their disturbing determination has lived on and has entered the world's languages. "Kamikaze" has long since become an everyday concept. Whenever a doomed undertaking is in the offing—be it in the political or economic realm, or even in the private realm of individuals—"kamikaze" is the term invariably chosen. To say that someone is "on a kamikaze mission" is to imply that they have no chance of winning, that the whole enterprise is futile. Throughout the world the name has become a byword for suicide, destruction, and fanaticism. Thus Muhammad Atta and his accomplices on September 11 immediately entered public consciousness as "kamikaze pilots."[6]

The word "kamikaze" actually means "wind," or, to be more precise, "divine wind." In the year 1281 such a wind, in the form of a typhoon, had struck the fleet of the Mongol Kublai Khan, grandson of Ghengis Khan, and sent it to the bottom of the Sea of Japan. Kublai Khan, bent on conquering Japan, lost more than 100,000 men to the savage wind, according to legend.

In contrast to the divine wind from which they took their name, however, the kamikaze pilots of World War II were incapable of turning the tables. The majority of the attacks, though fatal for the pilots, were a complete failure. The pilots were either shot down, crashed prematurely, or else simply missed their target because of inadequate flying skills (most of the pilots had received only a few hours' training before being sent on their missions). It seems that only between one and three percent of the thousands of kamikaze pilots actually managed to strike an enemy ship.[7]

Why, then, did thousands of young Japanese in the prime of their life (or even younger) not resist superiors who sent them off to certain death? Why did some of them actually volunteer for such missions even when it had long since become clear that the war was as good as lost? The answer lies in the depths of the popular mentality of imperial Japan, with its tradition of the samurai and the ethical code that goes with it, the *bushido* (*bushi* = warrior, *do* = way, method). The great classic of samurai literature, *Hagakure,* first published in 1716, begins with the pronouncement "The way of the samurai manifests it-self in death," its central argument being that only a samurai who is willing to die can truly serve his lord.[8] Without endorsing the popular notion of an eternal samurai mentality in Japan, we can justifiably say that during the war years, and especially among the military, this cultural heritage played a key role in providing an authoritarian regime the means to demand unconditional devotion to the cause, including the willingness to throw away one's life. Anyone who was attached to life was in consequence not prepared to die for his emperor, and was therefore considered a poor soldier.

Also essential to the kamikaze ideology is the legend of Kusunoki Masahige, the loyal samurai of Emperor Go-Daigo (1294–1336).[9] Masahige was a brilliant general whose first great deed was to help his lord to drive the Hojo shogunate from power in 1333 and thus enable him to establish a regime modelled after the exemplary reign of Emperor Daigo (897–930). Soon after this victory, Masahige faced a challenge from Ashikaga Takauji, a general who had previously been loyal to Emperor Go-Daigo, but who switched sides and led his troops against the emperor's forces.

With Takauji's troops advancing ever nearer to Kyoto, the seat of the emperor's power, Masahige suggested fleeing temporarily to the Holy Mountain of Hiei and abandoning the capital to the enemy. Later, and with the help of the monks, he would swoop down from the Holy Mountain and destroy the enemy—a ploy he had already used successfully on numerous occasions. But the Emperor refused to quit the city and insisted on the set-piece battle. In a final act of absolute obedience, Masahige bowed to the emperor's command—even though this meant certain death for both him and his troops. The Battle of Minatogawa in July 1336 turned into an utter disaster, and Masahige, completely surrounded by the enemy, committed suicide, together with 600 of his soldiers. According to legend, he cried out as he died: "If only I had *seven* lives to give up for my country!"[10]

Masahige is regarded as the perfect embodiment of the *bushido* code of honor. The story of his noble self-sacrifice was included in the national curriculum taught in Japanese schools in the years prior to the Second World War, so that in 1944 every young person in Japan was familiar with the legend of Masahige, the hero who died an honorable death.

This legend, together with the whole mental world of the samurai and the strict rules of *bushido*, played a decisive role in the education meted out to the kamikaze pilots both before and during their military service. From infancy onwards, all Japanese children in imperial Japan learned to regard the emperor as a living god, and to regard war as a process that could purify them, their nation, and ultimately the entire world. In this worldview, the valiant surrender of one's own life appeared as the purest form of self-fulfilment as well as a patriotic duty.

It soon became blindingly obvious to the young kamikaze pilots that neither they nor their aircraft had the slightest influence on the course of the war—but this recognition had practically no effect on the general determination to continue along the same path. It may seem paradoxical to us, but within the Japanese tradition as it was manifest in imperial Japan, it was precisely this recognition of inevitable defeat that egged on the young pilots. In his study of suicide in Japan, the French japanologist Maurice Pinguet concluded that promises of heavenly salvation played no role for the pilots: "They hoped neither for reward, nor for Paradise. In the end they didn't even hope for victory." And every death produced further deaths: "The more their comrades' death toll increased, the greater the determination of those that remained to follow their example, ashamed as they were of their attachment to life."[11]

Few survivors dared to speak of their fates, and only decades later—partly because they were afraid of being ostracized, but chiefly because of the shame and guilt they felt vis-à-vis their comrades who had perished in their aircraft. Consider the psychological environment in which they had grown up: a matrix that included esprit de corps, an inculcated habit of subordinating individual needs to those of the collective, and, for many, a sense of elation at being part of an élite. Loyalty to the emperor and obedience to the military were stronger than their emotional ties to family or friends. Describing his wartime perspective, one survivor remarked that he was "merely a speck of dust in the history of Japan."[12] The moral code that prevailed at that time is perhaps most clearly epitomized in the statement that "we were obliged to volunteer."[13]

And these young men did not shirk their obligations. How indeed could they have? The military was their whole world, and to refuse orders was simply inconceivable. The life of the kamikaze pilot was strictly ritualized from his first day of training to his final mission. The fixed daily routine, the ritual activities, the clear-cut rules and regulations were all designed to make the trainees appreciate that they were being subsumed into a special, more elevated tradition. Moreover, the sheer repetition and monotony offered a sort of comfort—after all, even those who know they are due to die cannot altogether turn their backs on the mundane routines of life.

With the end of the war in August 1945, the kamikaze pilots vanished as suddenly as they had appeared in 1944. But it was as if two separate strands in the history of suicide attacks had mysteriously conjoined when, in the first hours after the attacks of September 11, the Jordan bureau of the Associated Press received the first—and only—call claiming responsibility: a man speaking Arabic with a foreign accident declared that the "Japanese Red Army" had organized the attacks. "In revenge for Hiroshima," he said, then hung up and was never heard of again.

Absurd though this may seem—and absurd it was!—there has indeed been close cooperation over the past three decades between various radical Palestinian groups and the tiny, elusive, and extremely violent Japanese Red Army. Long before the Shi'ite Hezbollah and, later, the Hamas bombers got in on the act, the first suicide attacks in the Middle East were carried out by three Japanese gunmen: on May 30, 1972 they unleashed machine-gun fire in Israel's Ben Gurion International Airport near Tel Aviv, killing twenty-four people. They made no attempt to escape, and two of them were shot dead by airport guards.

That this was intended as a suicide attack was made crystal clear by the subsequent behavior of the sole survivor, Kozo Okamoto. Desperately unhappy to have ended up alive, he did his utmost to remedy this shameful state of affairs. He struck a bargain with one of the Israeli investigating officers, who promised to let him have his gun and a single bullet in exchange for a full confession. The officer got his confession, but Okamoto never got the gun; instead—to complete his shame—he received a life sentence. In 1985 he was exchanged, along with 1,150 Palestinians, for the Israeli soldiers abducted by the Popular Front for the Liberation of Palestine–General Command (PFLP-GC). He once again joined the Japanese Red Army, and sought shelter in Lebanon, where he was eventually given political asylum.

Okamoto and his two accomplices were not crazy mavericks running amok for their own private purposes, but the last remnants of the radical Japanese left. In the 1960s they had mobilized hundreds of thousands in protest first against Japan's security treaty with the United States, and then against the entire political establishment. But following the storming and occupation of universities in Tokyo and other cities, the vast majority of protesters resumed their middle-class lives. A tiny group decided to carry on and intensify their protests through armed struggle, however, and went underground in 1970. Sekigun, the Japanese Red Army, was born, intent on starting a world revolution.

The Red Army's plan was to shake Japanese society out of its lethargic state by the use of pamphlets, comics, films—and explosives. Bomb attacks and murders shook the country, members acting on the belief that if they ratcheted up their violence to a sufficient level, a revolution would certainly be triggered. The group soon split into splinter groups. The "Home Sekigun" spread terror across the land; then in the winter of 1971–72 its members holed up in mountain huts near Nagano, where after a ten-day battle with police the remaining five were captured in February 1972.[14] Even as the battle was going on, the police discovered fourteen corpses in the immediate area: over a period of time the two leaders had given orders for most of the group to be stabbed, beaten, or tortured to death.

A second splinter group, the "International Sekigun," left Japan in 1971 and found a new beachhead for starting world revolution: the rebellious Palestinians in southern Lebanon. Their members, too, are now almost all in jail. The last of those jailed, Fusako Shigenobu, one of the leaders, was captured in November 2000 near Osaka, having entered the country with false papers.[15]

This group's apocalyptic successors in the 1990s, the sect calling itself *Aum Shinrikyo* ("supreme truth"), no longer had any conventional political aims at all. The near-blind guru Asahara assured his followers that "only those who destroy the world can save it." As Haruki Murakami noted, theirs was a "language and logic cut off from reality" that had "a far greater power than the language and logic of reality."[16] On the morning of March 20, 1995, five members of Aum boarded subway trains in Tokyo carrying packages containing the nerve gas sarin. Before leaving the trains they pierced the sealed sarin packages with the sharpened tips of their umbrellas. Twelve people died and nearly 5,000 were injured. In this instance the term "cowardly terrorism" is apt, for while the poisoners of Aum Shinrikyo had dedicated themselves to the destruction of humanity, they had taken great care to ensure that they themselves would not be included. This concern for their own escape and survival is one of the main reasons why the death toll was not much higher.

The Parasites of Anger

AL-QAEDA AND THE ISLAMIST *INTERNATIONALE*

❈

The Americans love Pepsi-Cola. We love death!
—a young Taliban fighter

The storms of Paradise are on the move!
—war cry of *Ichwan* ("Brothers"), an early-twentieth-century
radical Islamic movement based in Saudi Arabia

On the morning of November 20, 1979, long before the world had ever heard of al-Qaeda, a group of 400 heavily armed Saudi extremists occupied the supreme Islamic shrine in Mecca. Led by Juhaiman al-Utaibi, a former Saudi National Guard soldier,[1] the men barricaded themselves in the gigantic complex. They called themselves *Ichwan,* brothers, in homage to the legendary warriors of Ibn Saud, the early twentieth-century founder of the kingdom, and rejected the Saudi monarchical regime as hypocritical and heretical. Al-Utaibi had proclaimed himself the *Mahdi,* the returned Messiah, and demanded, among other things, a ban on television and soccer. The Saudi army eventually had to enlist elite foreign troops to end the occupation, and several hundred people lost their lives in the process. The last sixty-three surviving occupiers were executed in January 1980.[2]

One might expect that since this bloody episode occurred in 1979, the year of the Islamic Revolution in Iran, the Ayatollah Khomeini was somehow involved. And indeed, Khomeini did want to use Iran as a base from which to incite the entire Islamic world to rise up against their rulers and the West. Ultimately, though, the Shi'ite fury remained restricted to the Shi'ite world. The brief Sunni uprising in Mecca was more directly related to another fateful event of that year: the Soviet invasion of Afghanistan. Afghans and volunteers from across the Arab world came together as mujahideen, as jihad warriors, to fight the infidel occupier. The Americans, as a rival imperial power, had every interest in helping to organize the initially uncoordinated resistance and funding a proxy war against their Cold War rival. So the mujahideen were provided with weapons, including Stinger antiaircraft missiles, technical support, and cash.

Financial assistance also flowed toward the mujahideen from the oil-rich kingdom of Saudi Arabia. Saudi Arabia had been unsettled by the Islamic Revolution; it had a restive, aggrieved Shi'ite minority to deal with, and once in power the Ayatollah Khomeini did not delay in making a barely disguised appeal for the toppling of the "corrupt dynasty." The Saudi royal family felt a strong need to bolster its Islamic credentials and prove to the Islamic world that it, too, was capable of waging a principled religious struggle. One serious obstacle facing them, however, was the fact that no one in Saudi's leading families was prepared to swap his comfortable life for a rough—indeed, mortally dangerous—existence in Afghanistan. Until Osama bin Laden.

There was great delight in the Saudi kingdom when Osama bin Laden, until then a rather unremarkable scion of one of the country's wealthiest aristocratic families, set off for the town of Peshawar in western Pakistan, the center of the mujahideen resistance. He and his mentor, Abdullah Azzam, founded the *Maktab al-Khidamat* or "Services Office,"[3] a recruitment office for Islamic *internationalistes* prepared to fight the communist infidels.[4] The governments of the countries of origin of these fighters weren't especially sorry to see these troublemaker-idealists go, and handed them exit visas without any fuss. Thus began the globalization of Islamist terrorism—born in the Afghan-Pakistani frontier as a joint venture, with the help of

Western and Arab midwife governments having all kinds of vested interests in the phenomenon.

✦

The alliance between the Americans and the Islamists was fated to end a decade after it began. The American government lost interest in its mujahideen allies after the Soviet retreat from Afghanistan in 1989. The Islamists, for their part, were outraged when half a million American troops were allowed into Saudi Arabia after Saddam Hussein's 1990 invasion of Kuwait. (The Saudi royal family had granted the Americans permission to use the kingdom as a base of operations against Iraq—and to protect the Saudi oil fields.) Osama bin Laden had approached the royal family with an offer to create a new Islamic defense force for the kingdom from the thousands of mujahideen who had returned from Afghanistan, but he was rebuffed. The Kingdom preferred to receive its protection from Saddam Hussein from the Americans' high-tech war machine. Bin Laden was left with a large fighting force with nothing to do—a sect waiting for a new opportunity to battle infidels—and with a powerful grievance against a corrupt Saudi government that allowed infidels to send its soldiers into the land of Islam's holiest sites. Thus was born al-Qaeda, a shadowy organization with a structure as opaque as its Arabic name, which can be loosely translated as "the basis" or "the base."

In the case of al-Qaeda, unlike Islamic Jihad or Hamas, it is difficult to find individual cadres who readily identify themselves as members. Nor does the group feature a communications office issuing manifestos and other policy pronouncements. The upshot is that it is almost impossible to discover who exactly is behind an attack, and how the chain of command operates. (If indeed there is a chain of command: Bin Laden has been described as "more an inspirer than a commander" by a member of an investigative team from the *New York Times*.)[5] Al-Qaeda's goal, at once crystal clear and completely vague, is to hit the West wherever and whenever it can, in order to further polarize the Muslim and Western worlds and effect an eventual victory of the Islamists (who claim leadership over the Muslim world). Osama bin Laden's famous fatwa in 1998 exhorted Muslims to join in a supposedly defensive jihad for the protection of Islam and Muslim territory against "Jews and Crusaders." Muslims everywhere, he said, were under attack from the "troops of the Crusaders" who are "spreading like crickets"—in the "occupation" of Saudi Arabia, in the "continuing aggression against the Iraqi people," and in particular, in the "occupation" of Jerusalem by "the meaningless state of the Jews." The 1998 fatwa was in effect a call to total, unconditional war, with all devout Muslims commanded to "kill the Americans and their civilian and military allies alike." Just to make sure that his intended audience would understand the sweeping nature of these injunctions, he added that this "is a duty for every single Muslim in a position to do so and, indeed, in every country where it is possible to carry it out."[6]

After beginning its operations in 1992 with conventional bomb-planting methods,[7] al-Qaeda graduated to suicide bombings on a large scale when, on August 7, 1998, two delivery trucks loaded with explosives blew up within minutes of each other outside the American embassies in Nairobi, Kenya and Dar es Salaam, Tanzania. Although the attack could have been much worse—neither driver-assassin succeeded in manoeuvering his TNT-laden truck directly beside embassy buildings—the explosions killed a total of 224 people, including twelve Americans, and injured more than 4,300.

Although the masterminds of these attacks have thus far eluded police and intelligence services worldwide, some information about the planning of the Nairobi attack has come from a less fortunate, lower-level operative. Saudi citizen Muhammad Rashed Daoud Al-Owhali was meant to have died in the passenger seat of the exploding truck. His assignment had been to shoot the guard posted at the compound gate and open the gates so as to gain entry to the embassy grounds. But at the last minute, the hapless Al-Owhali realized that he'd forgotten his pistol. He jumped out of the truck, threw a hand grenade at the guard, and ran away, while the driver raced towards the gate and detonated his fatal freight on impact.[8] Al-Owhali was taken to the hospital along with the other injured, but the ammunition in his trouser pockets exposed him as an accomplice. Together with three other key players in the Nairobi attack, Al-Owhali was sentenced to life imprisonment in October 2001 in New York.

During the next few years after the 1998 Nairobi and Dar as Salaam bombings there were several planned attacks on Western targets that were successfully prevented, including one on the Strasbourg Cathedral,[9] one in the baggage claim area of Los Angeles International Airport, and another on Israeli tourists in Jordan.[10] There were also several retaliation bombings, including an ineffectual American sortie that destroyed a pharmaceuticals factory in Sudan on August 20, 1998, which had been mistaken for a chemical weapons production site; and an American rocket attack on an al-Qaeda training camp near the Afghan town of Khost on the Pakistani border, which killed several Pakistani Kashmir fighters who were training there. But al-Qaeda remained relatively quiet—until October 2000, when two men in a large, white, inflatable dinghy drew up alongside the American destroyer, the USS *Cole,* on a six-hour refuelling stop in the Yemeni port of Aden. Many of the 300-member crew of the ultramodern, 142 meter-long, billion-dollar battleship were having lunch or watching the Tom Cruise movie *Mission: Impossible* on the huge video screen in the mess when, at 11:18 a.m., the ship suddenly heaved upwards.[11] The men in the dinghy, who had given crew members on deck a friendly salute as they approached the ship, detonated 225 kg of explosive charges alongside the *Cole,* using a clever form of bomb construction that steered all the explosive energy in the direction of the ship.[12] The force of the explosion, which of course blew up the two bombers, very nearly snapped the battleship in two. Seventeen American sailors died, and forty were wounded.

In this case, a little boy provided the crucial clue to the investigators. A man had asked him to keep an eye on the car that had been used to take the dinghy to the water.[13] From this evidence, the path led to a network of "preparers" who had lived on and off in Aden for years, and to several men in positions of leadership in al-Qaeda, including Muhammad Omar al-Harazi, an explosives expert. But the Yemeni government has not gone out of its way to help the American investigation. The local accomplices were, after all, the same Yemeni veterans of the Soviet-Afghan war who filled the ranks of al-Qaeda, and who had helped Yemen's president Ali Abdullah Saleh in the civil war against the communist secessionists in the country's south. As for Osama bin Laden, he again did not claim direct responsibility, but neither did he deny being at least the guiding spirit behind the attack. In the summer of 2001, he arranged for the distribution of a video that begins with pictures of a little boat in Aden harbor, then features footage of the enormous hole in the USS *Cole*. The commentary, offered by Bin Laden himself, rejoices that "Allah gave us a victory today with the destruction of the ship."[14]

And then all went quiet again. In summer 2001, several television correspondents from various Arab countries were invited to Afghanistan and into al-Qaeda's camps, where they were allowed to film Bin Laden, although not to interview him. Before leaving, they were told that the Americans could expect a "major blow."[15]

The blow came on the morning of September 11, 2001, a day with bright blue skies on the American east coast—a perfect day for flying. At 7:45 a.m., American Airlines flight 11, a Boeing 767, took off from Boston's Logan Airport for Los Angeles. Thirteen minutes later, United Airlines flight 175 departed Logan for the same destination. At 8:01 a.m., United Airlines flight 93, a Boeing 757, took off from Newark International Airport, headed for San Francisco. And, finally, at 8:10, American Airlines flight 77 departed from Washington's Dulles Airport en route to Los Angeles. On board the four airplanes were nineteen hijackers, armed with sturdy box-cutters. Once the planes had reached cruising altitude, the hijackers seized control of the cockpits, while assuring the passengers that no harm would come to anyone. The story of what happened over the next few horrible hours scarcely needs to be told yet again. In the deadliest suicide attacks heretofore conceived, commercial passenger jets, fuel tanks brimming for transcontinental flights, were turned into gigantic guided missiles, aimed at the Twin Towers of the World Trade Center in

Manhattan and the Pentagon in suburban Washington, D.C. (A fourth planned target—unknown, but presumably a large and prominent government building in Washington, such as the White House or the Capitol—was missed after several passengers aboard United Airlines flight 93 put up a desperate cockpit fight with the hijackers, causing the jet to plunge into a field southeast of Pittsburgh, Pennsylvania.) By 10 a.m., more than 3,000 people had died: Americans for the most part, but also 200 British subjects and people of more than fifty other nationalities. Christians, Jews, and Muslims alike were among the victims.

No longer were suicide attacks a weapon used in faraway countries by small groups of radicals waging war on their own turf, or on the turf of their neighboring enemy, and driven by essentially parochial agendas. The tremendous repercussions of that terrible day, a day that changed the world, were many and varied, and will continue to be felt for many years. The attacks have led to two American-led wars, in Afghanistan in 2001 and in Iraq in 2003. (Plans for the latter may have been in place earlier, but could only be enacted in the highly charged, emotional post–September 11 political atmosphere, when the Bush administration successfully persuaded a majority of Americans that Sadaam Hussein was somehow linked to the al-Qaeda attacks.[16] The Twin Towers and Pentagon bombings also turned President Bush, who until then had widely been considered a mediocre, or at least indifferent, president, into a war hero in his own country and gave a tremendous boost to all of his administration's policies, foreign and domestic.

But the attacks also changed popular perceptions of al-Qaeda, too. By its spectacular and horrific *coup de théâtre*, al-Qaeda was vaulted in the eyes of world public opinion into a stratum far above groups such as Hamas and Hezbollah. For many, especially in Western countries, they became the very incarnation of terror, pure and simple, and Osama bin Laden became the embodiment of evil.

Since September 11, any al-Qaeda announcement made via videotape or sound recording and broadcast by the Qatar-based satellite channel Al-Jazeera forces Western governments to put their foreign embassy personnel on standby. Flights are canceled, and holiday resorts declared crisis spots. Whole armies of surveillance personnel go hunting for suspect telephone calls, financial transactions, couriers, or plans of attacks. But even with this tremendous expenditure of resources, the task is not easy. Since the loss of its territorial base in late 2001, al-Qaeda has reorganized itself from scratch, exchanging the relative stability and openness of a Taliban-dominated Afghanistan for a vast, clandestine, decentralized underground operation with cadres based in cities and towns across Asia and Africa.

This newly reconfigured network no longer requires centralized leadership. It can compensate for and replace murdered leaders because of its hermetic, internally undisputed worldview. One doesn't need a central command if the aims are clear; local cadres are free to take the initiative. Moreover, al-Qaeda's forceful, pan-Islamic ideology allows for an easy colonization of local centers of conflict throughout the Islamic world, existing groups with local grievances swearing allegiance to the pan-Islamic agenda and transforming themselves into offshoots. In this way, al-Qaeda operates like McDonald's: according to the franchise system. Wherever (Sunni) Muslims organize themselves into fighting groups, whether against foreign, "infidel," occupying powers or against Shi'ite neighbors, they are infiltrated by al-Qaeda men, who offer their know-how with respect to bomb making, poison manufacturing, guerrilla tactics, and obtaining financial aid. Since the end of major fighting in the U.S. war in Afghanistan, three new cases exemplify the speed with which al-Qaeda has secured new beachheads, even if the groups concerned act under their own names: Karachi, Pakistan; Iraqi Kurdistan in northern Iraq; and the Russian province of Chechnya.

There is nothing new about people in Karachi being murdered for their beliefs; but the situation was previously of no interest to the West because, up until a couple of years ago, local terrorist sects such as Lashkar-e-Jangvi confined themselves to murdering other Muslims who did not to share their religious persuasion. Shi'ites gunned down Sunnis, assassinating hundreds of doctors, lawyers, shopowners, and clerics. Sunnis, in retaliation, murdered Shi'ites. Since October 2001, however, the situation has changed. It began with the murder of sixteen people in the "American Church" in Bahawapur, central Pakistan, followed in January 2002 by the kidnapping and gruesome, videotaped murder and decapitation of the American *Wall Street Journal* investigative reporter Daniel Pearl. Four months later, in May and June 2002, two suicide attacks devastated Karachi: the first on a bus filled with French engineers in front of the Sheraton hotel, and the second on the grounds of the American consulate. A group named al-Qanun—"the law"—unknown up to then, admitted responsibility for both.

The al-Qaeda connection became clear to Pakistani authorities soon enough. In July 2002, according to a Pakistani secret serviceman,[17] officers from the Pakistani intelligence agency, ISI, arrested Sheikh Ahmed Salim in a covert operation. Salim is a Kenyan-born al-Qaeda officer who had been indicted in absentia in New York for having allegedly purchased the truck used by the suicide bombers who attacked the U.S. embassy in Nairobi in 1998. Salim, who had taken refuge in al-Qaeda camps in Afghanistan, fled to Karachi during the American bombardments and invasion in October 2001. After his capture, he told his Pakistani interrogators that al-Qaeda had succeeded in turning Asif Ramzi, the leader of Lashkar-e-Jangvi, into their tool. Apparently Ramzi was desperately seeking outside sponsors as a way of gaining the upper hand in an internal power struggle.[18] His group, up until then notorious for fatal shootings from moving cars, were initiated in the techniques of suicide attacks, and he himself had been persuaded henceforth to kill foreigners instead of Shi'ites. Asif Ramzi was, according to Pakistani investigators, behind the most recent attacks in Karachi.

Another of al-Qaeda's recent beachheads has drawn much more world attention, for obvious reasons. In the small, exceedingly remote and inaccessible mountain region of what had been, since the most recent Iraq war, the autonomous Kurdish enclave in northern Iraq, a radical group of Kurdish Islamists operating under the name of Jund al-Islam, or Army of Islam, had been engaged in low-level skirmishes with the nationalist Kurdish fighters of the PUK, or Patriotic Union of Kurdistan (also known as the Peshmerga, those "ready to die"), which controls the eastern half of Iraqi Kurdistan. In October 2001, about the same time when dozens of Arab veterans of the Afghani war against the Soviets fled the U.S. strike forces and took refuge in the Kurdish mountains, the group changed its name to the harmless-sounding Ansar al-Islam ("House of Islam" or "Partisans of Islam"), and simultaneously began a murderous guerrilla war against the PUK. Equipped with a huge supply of shells, they fired almost every night at the opposing front lines; in December 2002, they slaughtered forty-two captured PUK Peshmerga fighters with knives and axes, and, shortly afterwards, stabbed to death several high-ranking PUK officers whom they had lured into a trap. At the same time, they set up a rigid Kingdom of God, a kind of miniature version of the repressive Taliban regime in Afghanistan, where they banned the consumption of alcohol, as well as listening to music and CDs of all sorts (apart from recorded sermons), posted signs warning people to fear God, and had people who broke the rules publicly whipped. At the start of 2002, Ansar initiated its first of four suicide attacks: on February 26, a young man blew himself up at the edge of the Iraqi Kurdish town of Halabya, killing himself, a taxi driver, and two PUK soldiers. Many more people would have died if he had reached his target, the Iraqi Kurdish regional capital of Sulaymaniyah, but he panicked when approached by police. Three further such attacks took place in the following weeks, although only one attacker reached Sulaymaniyah, where he panicked and killed only himself.

My own investigations, conducted in the days following the capture of Ansar's hiding place by U.S. special forces and allied PUK troops after the American invasion of Iraq in March 2003, confirm the deep involvement of al-Qaeda in the activities of this group. Along with explosives were found collections of Islamist sermons, and instructions for making biological and chemical toxins as well as explosives—all copies of documents discovered months earlier in captured Afghan territory by American forces, in many cases with identical wording.[19] This evidence confirmed what Ansar members had already stated: that Ansar al-Islam had been created out of nothing by the Arab veterans of the struggle against the Soviet occupation of Afghanistan who had trickled in after October 2001.[20] The odd disconnect between the group's grandiose public declarations that it was fighting "Judaism worldwide" and the fact that it never got beyond attacking its local neighbors, was a sure sign of its recent colonization by al-Qaeda.

Chechnya has also become an important point on the global jihad map, and a magnet for Islamist fighters without jobs and, since the loss of Afghanistan in October 2001, with no base of operations. Everything fits here: Muslim nationalists fight for their country's independence from a Christian—indeed, heretical—occupying power that acts with the greatest cruelty. But it hasn't simply been several hundred Wahhabites—as the Chechens call the fighters who often come from Saudi Arabia—who are implicated in the struggle; the natives are, too.

The Chechens hate the Russians. They have wanted a state of their own for years, but the Russian government is keen to send a message to all minorities under its control that any attempt to leave the Russian federation, already considerably reduced from the former Soviet empire, will be severely punished. For the Russians, it is not so much about land—Chechnya is barely half the size of Switzerland—as about power, and, of course, maintaining access to gas and oil reserves around the Caspian Sea.

In the capital, Grozny, one can meet young Chechens every day who will tell you that they have lost a brother, a sister, one of their parents, in the course of the struggle for independence. The Russian occupation has exacted a terrible toll. Months of aerial bombardment have reduced large parts of the capital city to dust. Russian soldiers, by many accounts, have acted abominably—looting, abducting civilians, torturing and murdering suspected supporters of the independence movement with impunity. The young Chechen survivors vow to avenge every one of these murders, until all the Russians have gone. And the talk has led to action, in the form of suicide bombing.

For most of the young Chechen bombers in waiting, the rules of *Adat,* a traditional Chechen code of honor, are more important than any religious motive. Jihad is overshadowed by a desire to exact retribution for the sake of honor. The mixture of jihad talk and Adat make for an odd but potent brew. Here radical Sunni Arabs on the fringes of al-Qaeda, who themselves received the concept and practice of suicide bombing from Shi'ite groups, now pass it on to a culture steeped in old tribal rules, Russian education, and an Islam that only first reached the country in the eighteenth century.

Following September 11, Russia's president Vladimir Putin decided to demonstrate his contribution to the American-led war on terrorism by intensifying his repression of Chechnya. When Putin visited New York in mid-November 2001, he was no longer calling Chechnya a "stronghold of separatism" but instead an "international terrorist enclave." Putin's determination to crush the resistance was demonstrated during the terrible days of October 2002. On the evening of October 23, in the middle of a performance of the hit Russian musical *Nord-Ost* ("North-East") in a theater on Moscow's Melnikova Street, three dozen Chechen hostage-takers, including eight women, stormed the theater and took the entire audience of 800 hostage. Mostly masked and girded with explosives, they offered the Kremlin a choice: either retreat from Chechnya, or watch the hostage-takers blow themselves and all their hostages to pieces. After three days and two nights of negotiations—during which the Kremlin stalled for time, rather than seriously negotiated—Russian special military units shot gas pellets into the theater to immobilize everyone, and proceeded to shoot dead numerous hostage-takers. Unfortunately, the gas was so highly concentrated that 129 hostages died from asphyxiation right before the eyes of desperate doctors who had not been forewarned to expect poison victims, and who had been given no information about the kind of gas used. Nobody will ever be able to say whether the hostage-takers would have detonated their live bombs. They must have had several minutes to do so once the gas started creeping up—but they didn't.

"Next time," a relative of one of the hostage-takers told the *Süddeutsche Zeitung*'s Russian correspondent two months later, "there won't be any negotiating. The bombs will be set off straight away."[21] And this is precisely what happened:

- On December 27, 2002, fifty-seven people died when a truck loaded with explosives smashed through the barricades of the government building in Grozny and blew up moments later.

- On May 12, 2003, another explosive-packed truck, this time with three attackers, including a woman, smashed through the barrier and the concrete blockade in front of the state administration building in Znamenskoye. Although the guards opened fire, they were unable to stop it; fifty-nine people died.

- On May 14, 2003, two female attackers carrying bombs under their clothes blew themselves up at a celebration for Prophet Muhammad's birthday in Ilaskham-Yurt, east of Grozny, killing twelve (fourteen, according to some sources) people. Their target was presumed to be Ahmed Kadirov, chairman of the pro-Russian administration, because his Kremlin party "United Russia" had organized the event, although he wasn't present.

- On June 5, 2003, a young female suicide bomber killed at least eighteen members of the Russian air force when she blew herself up on a bus in Mosdock, North Ossetia, which was traveling with more than thirty people on board, on their way to work at the local military airport. The woman, who had signaled to board the bus, was wearing a nurse's white coat. According to witness statements she declared "God is great" before detonating the explosive right on the bus, the doors having already closed.[22]

The suicide attacks continue, following the same pattern, and defying all attempts to halt them. A growing number of women, the "black widows," are among the attackers. And nothing indicates that this is a war that can be stopped.

In May 2003, President George W. Bush, in a moment of euphoria after his military's apparently easy victory on the Iraqi battlefield, and still insisting (as he would until September 2003) on an unsubstantiated link between al-Qaeda and Saddam Hussein, declared: "Al-Qaeda is on the run. The group of terrorists who attacked our country is slowly but surely being decimated."[23] Bush's optimism turned out to be ill-founded, and Egyptian President Hosni Mubarak's warning in March of 2003 that the U.S.-led Iraq war would produce "100 new Bin Ladens" was soon borne out.[24] Suicide attacks of all sorts, which have multiplied disturbingly since September 11, began to erupt afresh after Bush's triumphant claim to have sent al-Qaeda "on the run." May 2003, was an especially bad month. On May 12, a truck loaded with five tons of explosives rammed into an administrative building belonging to the hated Russian secret service in Snamenskoye, a Chechen town thirty-eight miles northwest of the capital Grozny. Fifty-nine people, most of them civilians, died, including eight children. Hours later that same day, shortly before U.S. Secretary of State Colin Powell's official visit to Saudi Arabia, several attackers blew themselves up simultaneously in three different locations in the Saudi capital Riyadh. The most prominent target, the al-Hamra compound northeast of Riyadh, contained one of the most exclusive housing developments for western foreigners in the Saudi kingdom. The high walls and twenty-four-hour guards proved ineffective in this case. A total of thirty-five people died in the three attacks in Riyadh that day, including eight Americans and nine of the attackers.

Amid all the attention focused on these attacks, it went almost completely unnoticed that, forty-eight hours later, a coordinated phalanx of motorcycle riders threw twelve sets of explosive charges at Shell filling stations in the Pakistani city of Karachi. As if by miracle, no one was hurt. Also ignored by the Western media was the detonation of a bomb, the day after the Riyadh attacks, in a courtroom in the Yemeni town of Jibla, where an Islamist had, a week previously, being condemned to death for murdering three American missionaries. And that same day, Lebanese police prevented a bomb attack on the American embassy in Beirut. The world media also paid scarce attention to a series of concerted attacks in the Moroccan city of Casablanca, four days after the Riyadh attacks, which hit five different locations in the city simultaneously: a hotel, two buildings housing Jewish organizations, the Belgian consulate, and the "Casa de Espana," a favorite meeting place for the 2,000 Spanish expatriates in Casablanca. Forty-two people died, including the thirteen attackers.

These attacks, however loosely coordinated, sent a clear, sobering message: al-Qaeda is by no means beaten. It continues to seek out targets it can hit at any time, including "soft" targets such as hotels and nightclubs, even in the face of official terrorist alerts. Being driven out of Afghanistan (at least temporarily) didn't so much defeat Osama bin Laden's followers as drive them underground. What makes this relatively new, clandestine network so dangerous is its recipe for combining two formidable elements so as to create a uniquely deadly form of militant group: an uncompromising, seductive, Manichean worldview that attracts a cult-like following, and a set of real, local grievances and ethnic and/or religious conflicts waiting to be enflamed. Like a parasite, al-Qaeda moves between the conflicts in the Islamic world, deriving sustenance from genuine, often well-founded local anger and grievances.

The Bush administration's confident assertions that al-Qaeda is "on the run" were not simply premature—they were entirely wrong. It is certainly true that the network has limited resources, that its opportunities to strike are constrained by high security, and that it often cannot be in a particular place at a particular time. But the fact that, either on its own or with the help of local supporting groups, it was capable of striking such a rapid succession of blows in half a dozen places immediately after the fall of Saddam Hussein served as an impressive display to the world of its reach and effectiveness.

The American occupation of Iraq, rather than striking a blow against terrorism, as the Bush administration believes, actually provides fresh impetus for it. For if the best starting point for Osama bin Laden's aggressive variety of jihad consists of defending Muslim territory against foreign occupying troops, then the American occupation of Iraq would be about the best thing that could happen, from the movement's point of view. Now, instead of facing a rival in the form of a dictator who himself donned an Islamic mantle, al-Qaeda can attack an army of occupation that many suspect has invaded Iraq to secure the country's oil supplies for the United States.

Separatist Movements and Female Suicide Bombers

THE CASES OF SRI LANKA AND KURDISTAN

> These women were fully aware and fully desirous of being free women with an important message to pass on and who could be examples to all women the world over.
> —Kurdistan Workers' Party (PKK) leader Abdullah Öcalan, talking about the first female Kurdish suicide assassins, 1996

The young Tamil woman had dressed herself up in shining robes and placed flowers in her hair, as if she were about to celebrate some sort of feast-day. She was holding a garland of sandalwood, which, ostensibly, she, like all the other flower-bearing locals, wanted to drape around the neck of Rajiv Gandhi, forty-six-year-old son of the legendary Indira Gandhi, who was passing through this town in the southern Indian state of Tamil Nadu—home of approximately fifty-five million ethnic Tamils—on a campaign stop. Rajiv, India's prime minister from 1984 to 1989, was in this race to win back the prime ministership and Indian government, and all indications were that he was about to return triumphantly to power. The date was March 21, 1991.

When Rajiv Gandhi finally arrived and stepped onto the red carpet at 10 p.m., the waiting crowd charged towards him. A female bodyguard tried to restrain the large Tamil reception party, but Gandhi, whose mother and grandfather had already been victims of assassins, said, "Give everyone their chance." It was precisely this chance that the young woman had been waiting for: she bowed down at Gandhi's feet and, with her right hand, detonated the explosive charge which she was carrying inside the custom-made vest concealed under her sari. In order to be absolutely sure of success, mission planners packed an enormous amount of explosive in that vest. There was little left of Gandhi's body after the blast.[1]

With the suicide assassination of Rajiv Gandhi—quite likely in revenge for Gandhi's decision as prime minister in the mid-1980s to dispatch Indian troops to Sri Lanka—the Tamil rebels in the Sri Lankan civil war bombed their way onto the world stage as a resolute and merciless fighting force.[2] For some twenty years, the rebel organization, the "Liberation Tigers of Tamil Eelam" (LTTE), has been engaged in a ruthless, uncompromising struggle for an independent homeland, called "Ealam" by the Tamils, on the island state of Sri Lanka. Their orientation was well described by a cabinet minister from the capital city of Colombo and member of the ruling Sinhala majority: "We fight in order to live. They fight in order to die."[3]

The attack on Gandhi was just one of countless suicide operations that have been carried out by the "Black Tigers," a specially trained elite unit of the LTTE in existence since the early 1980s. In July 1987, in a carbon copy of the Hezbollah suicide assault on the American marine barracks in Beirut, a Black Tiger blew himself up along with forty government soldiers after ramming an explosive-laden truck into a military camp. In 1991, two months before Gandhi's murder, Sri Lanka's defense minister was blown up by a harmless-looking cyclist. The LTTE also successful targeted Sri Lankan President Ranashinge Premadasa in 1993, who fell victim to a man who had successfully infiltrated the president's inner circle and had spent a year in his orbit before carrying out his mission. Premadasa's successor, Chandrika Kumaratunga, survived an attack in 1999, though he lost an eye. The list of high-ranking army officers and politicians assassinated over the years—including members of the ruling circle prepared to make compromises—is long. By 2000, the LTTE had carried out a total of 168 suicide attacks, killing more than 500 people and injuring thousands.[4] Their intention, it seems, was nothing less than eradicating Sri Lanka's ruling elite.

Successive Sri Lankan governments have carried out decades of apartheid policies, based on the assumption that the best way to deal with the minority Tamils—who make up between twelve and seventeen percent of the population and are concentrated in the island's north and east—was to subjugate them militarily. But these policies had the unintended effect of creating a monster. "The only way we can get our 'Tamil Eelam' is with weapons. It's the only way we'll get anyone to listen to us," claimed eighteen-year-old Vasantha, whose confession appeared in one of the rare interviews with the Tamil Tigers.[5] "This is the greatest sacrifice I can make. Even if I have to die in the process." The Sri Lankan civil war has been characterized by a merciless spiral of violence born of discrimination against a minority, whose militants fought back so viciously that the ruling party's army has been repeatedly provoked into revenge attacks. After almost twenty years of fighting, 65,000 people have died and a further 1.6 million displaced from their homes.[6]

Although there is no shortage of oppressed minorities in other parts of Asia—the Aceh peoples of North Sumatra, the Tibetans, and the Timorese of the island of East Timor in the Indonesian archipelago come to mind—none of them resort to the ultimate weapon of the suicide attack. Why does it happen in Sri Lanka? Ultimately, all attempts at explanation come back to legendary LTTE founder Vellupillai Prabhakaran. Within the LTTE organization, different units are responsible for training and for planning various kinds of attacks and suicide missions; but ultimately it has always been Prabhakaran alone who decides on strategy, executions, and suicide candidates. Prabhakaran's control over his organization is absolute and unquestioned, no doubt due in no small measure to the mythology that has arisen around him. He has supposedly tortured himself in order to toughen himself up, by inserting splinters under his fingernails and by spending hours lying in a sack in the sun.[7] Just as important as the legend, however, is his track record. Three decades of experience in guerrilla warfare has turned him into a brilliant strategist, and this, combined with an unerring instinct for power and a boundless faith in himself and his own righteousness, has allowed him to build up an army in the Sri Lankan jungles that operates more like a religious sect than a professional fighting force.[8]

The seeds of the Tamil-Sinhalese conflict were sown a century ago. The original Tamil of Sri Lanka were plantation workers who had been brought into Ceylon from India by the British starting in the mid-nineteenth century. After the British granted their former colony Ceylon its independence in 1948, the Sinhala majority—currently about three-quarters of Sri Lankan's population—seized political power, refusing all power sharing with the Tamil. The Sinhala majority even removed basic civil rights to the Tamils, in retribution for the perceived favoritism accorded to the Tamils by the British during the colonial period. When Sri Lanka severed its last formal ties with its former British colonial master and proclaimed itself a republic in 1971, the rights of the Tamil population were reduced still further. Resistance grew against the escalating discrimination and became increasingly militant. Student groups with a Marxist bent arose, the forerunners of later rebel organizations. More moderate Tamils founded their own party, the Tamil United Liberation Front (TULF). But all shared the same aim: to create a Tamil homeland, the idea of which is encapsulated in the phrase "Tamil Eelam." By this time many well-educated Tamils had fled abroad, and over 40 percent of those who remained were unemployed. It was an ideal breeding ground for the resistance fighters, and rebel organizations rapidly attracted significant support. By the mid-1980s, around twenty rebel organizations with 3,000 armed fighters dotted the landscape; the LTTE, founded in 1976, already had a fighting force of 1,500.

By the summer of 1983, after the majority's autocratic rule had reached the point where the moderate TULF was driven out of the national parliament, the Tamils' revolt had already become radicalized. On July 23 the LTTE aimed its first military blow at the government troops, killing thirteen soldiers. This operation unleashed savage reprisals on the Tamil population, as enraged Sinhalese killed hundreds of people with the knowledge and tacit consent of the Sinhala-dominated police.[9] Shan, then a 20-year-old student, had to watch as an old man was burnt alive before his very eyes. "That's when I decided to learn how to shoot back," recounted the future resistance fighter.[10] Even moderate Tamils began to sympathize with the armed rebels. Singham, a Tamil who fled to Germany as a student in 1984, clearly recalls the explosive atmosphere. "I didn't have anything to do with the LTTE, but that didn't make a bit of difference." At that time, the soldiers just arrested young Tamils quite arbitrarily, then locked them up and tortured them—only then did they became "terrorists." Fired up by hatred of the soldiers and the state, they attached themselves to the "Tamil Tigers."[11]

In this highly charged atmosphere, the opportunistic and savvy LTTE leader, Velupillai Prabhakaran, seized the opportunity to become the sole leader of the resistance and the "Tamil cause." On April 29, 1986, the LTTE unleashed its forces on the second largest paramilitary resistance movement, the Tamil Eelam Liberation Organization (TELO), overran all their camps, and killed two hundred TELO fighters, including their entire leadership. Thereafter Prabhakaran's organization assumed unrestricted supremacy on the Tamil side. Henceforth any Tamil who stood in their way was massacred as mercilessly as the hated Sinhalese enemy. And anyone reluctant to toe the line was brutally punished.[12]

In areas controlled by the LTTE in northeast Sri Lanka, the organization demands that at least one child from every Tamil family become a soldier. If the children refuse to freely present themselves, they are conscripted, taken from their homes, from schools, or just picked up in the streets. The Tigers have not been above snatching fourteen-year-olds from their beds under cover of darkness and carting them off to paramilitary camps.[13] This sort of coercion is, however, rarely necessary. Many choose to comply, having been raised on patriotic, mystical stories, songs, and films about the great Tamil freedom fighters. Young volunteers join up for many different reasons. Some hope to improve their miserable economic situation and, at the same time, their family's social prestige; others seek retribution for the abuse or murder of parents, siblings, or friends who were likely attacked before their very eyes.

Brainwashing methods have played a significant role in the Tamil Tiger organization. In its training camps, one hears heroic songs blaring from loudspeakers from dusk to dawn. LTTE recruits are not allowed to marry: they are already married to the "Tamil Eelam." Nor are they allowed to have sex,[14] for anyone who is chaste and who saves his sperm bestows a magical potency on it or gives it superhuman powers which are then set free at the critical moment.[15] The highest goal, drummed repeatedly into the heads of the youths, is to be ready to die for the common cause. "The greatest disgrace is to be caught alive by the enemy," teaches their leader Prabhakaran, and the highest honor is to be invited by him to a "last supper"—an opulent meal normally available only to those who have been chosen for a suicide attack.[16] As Hindus, the Tamils don't look forward to the prospect of a paradise "beyond." While Muslim suicide bombers often express confidently in their testaments that they will soon be taking their places at God's side in Paradise, the focus here is on the privilege of being at the side of God's chosen one in the here-and-now, for the first and last time, at an evening feast.

Like the bombers of Hamas, Hezbollah, and al-Qaeda, the earnest young men and women dispatched on suicide missions by the LTTE are posthumously honored. Scented candles, garlands of flowers, and papier-mâché effigies of the dead decorate their shrines. Their bodies—patched up, if possible—are carried to the funeral in a triumphal procession.[17] Part of this colorful posthumous fame benefits the individuals' relatives as well: instead of grieving for the dead, they can celebrate the heroism of a "Black Tiger" who achieved the aim of his mission. It's all a question of family honor.

While the very idea of a female suicide bomber causes great consternation for many in the Islamic world, among the Tamils a full one-third of the estimated 10,000 active Tiger cadres are women and girls.[18] And among the smaller subset of suicide commandos, female participation is even higher—close to sixty percent. Thus the modern emancipation of Tamil women has, in the political context of Sri Lanka, led to their being accorded the same rights and military duties as men in the struggle for Tamil independence. Female units have been included in battles since 1984, and Tamil Tiger training camps for women have been in place since 1987, with the first woman commanding a rebel unit in 1990.

It is highly doubtful that this high rate of women's participation in bombing missions has had much to do with a commitment to a Western form of feminism. More likely, it is because of the LTTE leadership's constant need for new blood. Many Tamil men of fighting age have died or emigrated. The few still available have been needed for combat duty against the government troops. Men are deemed more suitable for combat, being able to march greater distances while carrying heavier weapons, but women more easily conceal bombs under their clothes by, for example, passing themselves off as pregnant. It's a division of labor by gender: the exploding belt worn by suicide assassins, which the LTTE has managed to perfect over the years, was even originally developed specially for the female body.[19]

In its deployment of suicide bombers, the LTTE aim is not to terrorize the population as a whole with random attacks (in the way that, say, Hamas wreaks havoc in Israel), but rather to target with utmost precision the nerve center of the Sri Lankan state—either through attacks on decision makers or on the most susceptible weak spots in the infrastructure. The Black Tigers have destroyed, among other things, the headquarters of the state special armed forces unit, oil reserves in Kolonnawa, and the "Temple of the Tooth," an important Buddhist shrine prized by the Sinhalese. A particularly heavy blow fell on July 24, 2001, when the rebels effected a spectacular strike on Colombo International Airport. Although the plan didn't entirely come off, their aim was achieved: by damaging or destroying thirteen civil and military airplanes, they not only paralyzed the island's sole international air connection[20] but simultaneously destroyed half of the Sri Lankan air force and, perhaps even more significantly, caused long-term damage to the island's image as an idyllic holiday resort.

Up until quite recently, the LTTE has received support for its program—estimated at approximately one million dollars per month, in cash donations and weapons delivery[21]—primarily from among the half million Tamil exiles living abroad in the West.[22] But the organization also maintains good contacts with other separatist movements and terrorist groups. In the 1970s, LTTE fighters were already training together with the PLO. More recently, it has not been entirely clear to what extent Islamist groups have influenced or provided training for LTTE suicide attacks. There have been reported contacts between LTTE explosives experts and al-Qaeda and its mujahideen precursors since 1986, although the link has not been proven.[23] But Islamist influences have undoubtedly been manifest in less direct ways, especially through extensive global television and radio coverage of the deadly and successful Hezbollah attacks of 1983, and other, more recent and effective missions in the Middle East and elsewhere. Indeed, influence may pass in both directions. At least that is what the LTTE's commander of sea operations Soosai, claimed with respect to Al-Qaeda's successful bombing of the USS Cole in Yemen, which he saw as an imitation of a Tamil Tiger attack on a Sri Lankan marine warship in 1991.[24]

Suicide attacks have proven to be a most effective weapon in the Tamil Tiger arsenal, going a long way to compensate for the rebels' numerical inferiority and paucity of weapons technology. By 2000, the rebels had fought government forces to a complete standstill. Norwegian diplomat Eric Solheim, who took on the task of international mediation between the two civil war parties in November 2000, was quite open about it: "Neither side can win by military means."[25] As international pressure to negotiate a cease-fire increased, the government had no choice but to reverse its earlier, uncompromising policies, and hammer out a ceasefire agreement with the rebels that took effect in February 2002. It should be noted, however, that pressures for a ceasefire were not only being felt on the government side. In the post–September 11 atmosphere, after the launch of the American-led war on terrorism, international pressure also increased on the rebel side. Tamil organizations in the United States, Canada, and Great Britain were banned and money transfers from Tamil expatriates blocked by those countries' governments. Eager to reinvent himself as a statesman, LTTE leader Prabhakaran is now downplaying the suicide bombing tactic, and presenting himself as a man of peace. He wants his group to be recognized as a "freedom movement fighting for the oppressed Tamil people"[26] and, thus, as a legitimate and civilized negotiating partner, worthy of power-sharing—a form of recognition that is difficult to imagine the Sinhala side according, given the bitterness and hatred of recent times. Yet the combination of military success, increased international pressure, and a drop in funding from abroad have had an impact. The LTTE has renounced its demand for a separate, Tamil-dominated state, and is now prepared to accept Tamil territorial and political autonomy over the territory it controls—within a federal Sri Lanka. For the time being, the LTTE has stopped using suicide attacks, and as of this writing (November 2003) the February 2002 cease-fire agreement between the LTTE and the government is still holding.

Thousands of miles from the lush, green, tropical island of Sri Lanka is Kurdistan, a dry, dusty, and mountainous territory in the southeast of Turkey with a different religion and different cultural and political traditions. And yet, it is as if the same play were being remounted on a foreign stage. The Kurdistan Workers' Party (PKK) seems eerily like a copy of the LTTE. Like the Tamil Tigers, it arose in the 1970s in the midst of a conflict between an ethnic minority and the majority population, and escalated following the same pattern: the minority rebelled, and the majority hit back—with the destruction of Kurdish villages, the forced exile of Kurdish leaders, and the banning of books published in the Kurdish language. And as in Sri Lanka, the rebellious minority was radicalized rather than cowed by majority repression, until the whole minority population—Kurdish in this instance—fell in with the resistance movement against the overweening Turkish state. (The PKK rose in the 1980s to become the sole political voice of Kurdish nationalism, in no small measure because of the Turkish government's decision to ban all legal political parties in Turkey in the wake of a military coup in 1980.)

The two movements resemble each other in other ways as well. Their members are completely beholden to their leaders, sworn in as if into a sect, and adhere to a rigidly maintained hierarchical chain of command in which internal dissent is punished swiftly and severely. Indeed, the PKK soon mimicked the extreme centralization of the Turkish state, and became as true to the motto of the state's founder Ataturk as his national successors: "Revolution and mobilization from above."[27] Even the biographies of the respective strongmen have similarities. Like the Vellupilai Prabhakaran, Abdullah Öcalan was an indifferent university student, studying political science at the University of Ankara, before taking the path of the guerrilla fighter and faction leader.

Furthermore, in yet another deadly parallel between the PKK and the Tamils, a significant proportion of each organization's suicide brigade is made up of women.[28] The PKK discovered early on the great advantages of recruiting women—who, by taking part in the guerrilla war, were fighting not only for the liberation of their country but also for themselves. Born into Kurdistan's traditional, arch-conservative society, in which girls are literally sold to their husbands and bigamy and marriage between relatives are still normal practice, women play very circumscribed roles, looking after the children, the household, and the animals. Although Turkish law mandates primary school education for girls, many Kurdish women remain illiterate—not least because the PKK has a habit of killing teachers assigned to Kurdistan by the central government. (Teachers have not been well thought of because their instruction of Turkish is thought to dilute the children's Kurdish identity.)

Within the PKK infantry, by contrast, women were accorded equal rights with men. They had to complete the same training regimen and fight alongside the men—which would have been unthinkable in the traditional world of village life. Fighting in the PKK offered young female Kurds an escape from the prison of their traditional existence. But in casting their lot with this group, the women exchanged their traditional prison for a more treacherous form of imprisonment: once they had been chosen for a martyr operation, there was no escape. The most famous case is that of seventeen-year-old Leyla Kaplan, a PKK recruit who blew herself up in November 1996 in front of the headquarters of the police special forces in the South Turkish capital of Adana, killing three policeman. Another female PKK combatant, Turkan Adiyaman, had previously been asked to volunteer. After she refused, she was shot in front of Leyla Kaplan, as an example of the fate that befalls shirkers. This episode gives the lie to PKK leader Öcalan's repeated claims that the perpetrators of the suicide attacks were acting entirely on their own initiative: "If I'd ordered them to do it, the attacks would have been a hundred times more violent. The women committed symbolic acts which I didn't order them to commit."

Like the Tamil Tigers, the PKK never promised its people a first-class ticket to heaven, and religion has not been a major part of the martyrs' motivations. But the cause and the devotion to the leader became a substitute religion, and considered holy. Nominally secular, the PKK constructed a hermetic world conforming to the will and designs of Öcalan, who was accorded quasi-divine status. Then, however, in February 1999, the worst possible thing that could befall a sect like this happened: Öcalan was abducted by a crack regiment of Turkish commandos in Kenya, after a harrowing chase through Europe and Africa. PKK subcommanders immediately launched suicide attacks in retribution, the first on March 4, 1999, followed by six further such attacks in the space of a month. The Turkish state was threatened with an apocalyptic campaign of revenge if it made good on its threat to condemn and execute the captured leader.

Suddenly, the central player in this deadly game decided that he no longer wanted to play. Even as PKK fighters lined up to kill themselves to ensure their leader *wasn't* killed, the great leader himself pulled back from martyrdom, and started talking about ending the civil war and initiating a peace process. Abdullah Öcalan, to the chagrin of his many Kurdish supporters, apologized in court to the families of the soldiers who had died in the civil war; admitted that the armed struggle had been a mistake; and offered his services as a mediator—provided his life was spared.

His public display led to an official PKK declaration on July 7, 1999 that suicide attacks would be renounced. This led to a great deal of confusion among the Turkish military as well as within the PKK itself. Turkish state leaders began asking themselves whether a live Öcalan or a dead one was of more use to them. Is it better, they wondered, to risk creating a martyr and give in to popular cries for his execution, or, in light of his sudden willingness to make concessions in order to save his own life, to spare him as an important negotiating partner from his jail cell? In the end, a compromise was effected. Öcalan was indeed sentenced to death by the Turkish courts, but the government promised to respect the judgment of the European Court of Justice, which formally rejects the death penalty. Thus was Öcalan's death sentence commuted to life imprisonment three years later, and the PKK's series of suicide attacks ended just as it had begun: with a decree by Öcalan.[29]

After Martyrdom

RECENT DEVELOPMENTS IN IRAN

If our system is to be an Islamic one, it has to submit to a
democratic order. For true faith is based on free will.
—Abdolkarim Soroush, Iranian philosopher and reformist Islamic thinker[1]

More than a dozen Iranians meeting at the airport on time?
Not likely! Even if they would have managed it, they'd have
been off to Hawaii instead.
—Iranian satirist Ibrahim Nabawi on why his compatriots couldn't
have been responsible for the attacks of September 11, 2001

I t wasn't easy to find Ahmed, the tailor's son from the city of Meshhed, who'd gone off to the Iran-Iraq front as a gung-ho fourteen-year-
old in 1986 and had returned home blind. It is the winter of 1998,
and in Iran there are tens of thousands like him. But scarcely anyone
wants to talk about their experiences. We found Ahmed quite by
chance, after spending hours cruising around town in a taxi. Our taxi
driver and Ahmed had been in the same unit; like Ahmed, the driver
had been a "mine-jumper," and he had escaped with seventeen pieces
of metal shrapnel in his body—which only became noticeable when
he got out of the taxi and led the way, his steps slow and trembling,
to Ahmed's home. "Talk to him!" insisted our driver. "God has tested
him more severely than He tested me."

Ahmed was sitting against the wall on a foam mattress, his walking stick within reach. He had a different interpretation of what had happened to him. The bullet that struck him between the eyes, severed his optical nerve, and lodged itself above his nose was, he now claims, a piece of good fortune: "If this hadn't happened, I'd have become a tailor just like my father and his father before him. As it is, the War Invalids' Foundation financed my studies, and now I'm a teacher." He is married and has two children. At the time that he had been dispatched to that minefield at the height of the Iran-Iraq War, however, he had wanted to die. Or had he? "Well," he equivocates, "when I was fourteen, I hadn't really given death any thought. I *had* thought about Paradise." Of the twenty-five children in his unit, only two survived: the taxi driver and Ahmed.

A couple of years after his return he felt some pressure build up in his nose; after blowing it, out came the projectile. Or so he claimed, as a bullet souvenir was passed round the room like a talisman. "What we did then was right," he insists. "Imam Khomeini had his reasons for ordering us to do it. Otherwise, it would all have been meaningless. It must have been right! Only, I do sometimes think it would be nice to see my children. And spring. I always liked almond trees, you know."

Apart from his government-financed education, Ahmed came out the loser—as did his country as a whole. The war ended in 1988 without Iran having made any appreciable gains after 1982, the year the country recaptured territory seized by Iraq in its initial surprise attack in 1980. And today, the surviving members of these childrens' suicide brigades are met not with pride but, at best, pity, and often with incomprehension and ignorance. Relics from a bygone age, the survivors are avoided by a society that no longer wants to remember the embarrassing excesses of the country's recent past. Indeed, the difficulty of even locating Ahmed and other former child soldiers like him is due to a widespread reluctance to call attention to this failed business with God—this creation of a generation whose step into martyrdom had been aborted. Having been promised paradise, Ahmed, our taxi driver, and many others like them, remain among us—as broken people and embarrassments for a society in evolution.

❧

Militant factions around the world who have availed themselves of suicide attacks as a weapon can broadly be divided into two categories. On the one hand, there are the closed groups organized like sects or cults, which allow their members no life outside the group, or which operate in such isolation from the population that a return is impossible. These groups, which effectively take life-or-death decisions out of the individual's hands, include the Japanese Red Army, the Kurdish PKK, and, to a considerable extent, the Tamil LTTE. Because of their insularity, catastrophic military defeat—for example, the arrest of the PKK's supreme leader Öcalan—can spell the end of the suicide attacks. The situation looks quite different with the other type of militant group, where suicide bombing operations are tolerated, and indeed applauded, by an entire society, as in Lebanon in the 1980s and 1990s and in the present-day Palestinian territories. These are cases where attacks come, so to speak, *from* the people *for* the people. As Israel has learned since the launch of the most recent intifada in 2000, combating such attacks militarily is extremely difficult—many would argue, ineffectual. For if an entire society is so inspired by the battle against an occupying or invading enemy that the struggle begins to count for more than life itself, targeted liquidations of suicide brigade leaders only serves to strengthen the resolve of such groups.

The Iran of the Khomeini years fell into this second category: a militant government dispatching suicide bombers against a hated invader to popular acclaim. But the Iran of today no longer fits the scheme. Socially, politically, and psychologically, the country is light-years from the besieged Islamic Republic of the early 1980s, when a martyr's death was society's highest honor, when a "fountain of blood" spewed out red water at Teheran's Behesht-e Zahra cemetery, and when the Ayatollah Khomeini lauded a thirteen-year-old who threw himself at a tank holding a hand grenade as the inspiring "true leader of Iran." The profound changes manifest in contemporary Iranian society are demonstrated nowhere more clearly than in the awkward, ambivalent dealings with the relatives of the war dead, with the survivors of the suicide brigades, and with the whole myth of the martyr. The modern cult of martyrdom, as we saw in chapter 2, began in Shi'ite Iran, with its Passion mythology of Imam Hussein's self-sacrifice for a just cause and the True Faith; but it's precisely here that this same cult has, twenty-four years after the Islamic Revolution, largely disappeared, in a manner almost without parallel elsewhere in the Islamic world.

The idea of killing oneself or, indeed, other people, in order to enter Paradise, is a completely alien conviction in today's Iran. When the news of the September 11 attacks reached Iran, it provoked a popular response unthinkable in Cairo, Karachi, or Beirut: spontaneously organized mass funeral processions for the victims. In other places in the Islamic world, too, horror far outweighed the *Schadenfreude* felt by some people at America's loss. But elsewhere the horror was accompanied by silence, and often by widespread murmurings that the Americans had only themselves to blame, and by those now infamous and grotesque conspiracy theories, according to which Israel was behind the attacks. (The rumor, spread swiftly from Morocco to Indonesia after September 11 and believed by millions, held that 4,000 Jews employed in the Twin Towers had been telephoned by the Zionists the day before the attack and told not to go to work the following day.) But in Iran, home of modern-day anti-American Islamic fundamentalism, the place where the phrase "Great Satan" had been coined, sympathy ruled the day. The very idea of such a barbarous attack was so alien, so far removed from the mentality of contemporary Iranians that the satirist Ibrahim Nabawi could offer his own, tongue-in-cheek reason why his compatriots couldn't be responsible for the attacks: "More than a dozen Iranians meeting at the airport on time? Not likely! Even if they would have managed it, they'd have been off to Hawaii instead."[2]

It's not simply that martyrs have disappeared from the Iranian political landscape; also gone is any organized Islamic mass movement that could provide a strong and stable social basis for suicide bombers. In states such as Egypt, Pakistan, and Algeria, fundamentalist movements obtain their robust levels of support because their radicalized political Islam is the people's only weapon against corrupt governments widely perceived to be (in most cases, not without reason) clients of the United States. In Iran, there was such a movement— twenty-four years ago. It overthrew the shah's regime, took power, and, in effect, put the country through a massive controlled experiment designed to answer the question: What happens when a state is ruled "Islamically," under a new constitution that accords all real political power to the clergy? What happens when the law of the land deems a satellite dish, a private party with an open bar, and even sex before marriage an attack on the state's authority?

For more than two decades, Iran conducted its experiment on itself in isolation, sustained by its oil revenues and its faith. And the result? The concentration of power in the hands of an unrepresentative, unpopular ruling clique stuck in a time warp. The mullahs ruling Iran are, with few exceptions, the revolutionaries of yore, whereas the vast majority demands not a Holy State, but a democracy. Ironically, what put an end to the utopia of the Islamic theocracy was not the sort of crushing military defeat of political Islam typically and fervently hoped for in the West, such has come to pass in states such as Egypt, Algeria, and Uzbekistan, whose police and military have executed hundreds of suspected or actual Islamists, and arranged for the extra-legal "disappearance" of thousands of others. Rather, it is the victory of political Islam that, after a period of profound disillusionment, turned the Iranian people into the most secular, modern society in the region.

Painful disillusionment ruined political Islam's promises of salvation in Iran more than any outside influence could ever have done. The end of the popular romance with Islamic theocracy came from within. "Islam is the solution," promised the mullahs in 1979. But a cleric-led government could not eliminate, or even diminish, poverty or unemployment, which, according to the Iranian government Labor

Ministry's own figures, is running as high as 28 percent for those under thirty, and the new leaders proved to be just as corruptible as the old ones. The moral dictatorship turned inspired believers into a jaded, disgusted, and fed-up populace. The Khomeini era's praise for and popular social acceptance of martyrdom was beaten down not by military means—the preferred (and not terribly successful) method of Israel and the United States vis-à-vis their Palestinian and al-Qaeda jihadist foes—but by the Islamic state's own limitations and contradictions.

Iranians have turned away from the dreary, pedantic successors to the late Khomeini and embrace their twice-elected president, Sayyed Muhammad Khatami, who retains the majority's esteem despite the severe limitations placed on this power by the Iranian revolutionary constitution, which allows the leading clerics to trump democratically elected representatives of the people. Since Khatami's first electoral victory in 1997, the radical clerics and oligarchs who form the real seat of power, and their bureaucratic servants, have tried everything to humiliate the president and undermine his policies. They have forced his closest companions out of office, as was the case with the former minister of culture Ataollah Mohajerani; arrested them, as they did Abdollah Nuri, former minister of the interior; or shot them, as they did Said Hadscharian, Khatami's strategist and planner, and former second in command of the secret service, who was permanently crippled by his would-be assassin's bullet. But these were empty victories for the oligarchs. Every one of these attacks simply boosted Khatami and his remaining cohorts into higher public esteem.

The current battle over the future shape of the Iranian state is as bitter and furiously fought as it is clandestine. Neither side dares to attempt squashing the other entirely: the reformers don't have the military might and would be deposed if they attempted a power play, while the clerics with real power would be faced with a civil war if they eliminated Khatami, which would remove the last vestiges of democratic legitimacy from the regime. "They're both in the same boat," is how seasoned commentator on Iranian affairs Navid Kermani puts it, "and they're both trying to keep each other off the rudder."[3]

The track record of Iran's Islamic Revolution is decidedly mixed. Corruption has thrived to a grotesque degree, but villages have gained electricity, water, and medical care. Citizens are forced to submit to repressive rules of conduct, and women must cover themselves from head to toe—a far cry from the shah's era, when women on the streets of Teheran didn't look much different from women in Paris or New York. On the other hand, the schools and universities that have been set up across the country are open to women, and have given a whole new generation the chance of a different life. Iranian women have moved into a world that was as remote from them before the revolution as walking through Teheran unveiled is today: the world of paid work. A woman who can read, write, study, and earn money has acquired something that no concealing veil can ever take away from her: independence, and a desire for more freedom.

The generation born during the early years of the revolution, who are now coming of age and who form a majority in the country (70 percent of Iran's population is under thirty), have withdrawn from the rulers. Behind closed doors of apartments and houses, behind the garden gates, another world opens up, a world of private freedom where people watch banned films, have the odd drink, dance, and celebrate. A whole generation has grown up in this split existence, living a quasi-normal, cosmopolitan life within the false one they must outwardly display. In Iran, doing things in a roundabout way and expressing criticism in muted, indirect, coded language have become an art form, a game of great virtuosity in which little is actually said and much is meant. This occurs when, for example, the mullah in the holy city of Qom, critical of the ruling clerics, "praises" Iran's theocratic system by comparing it "Plato's Utopia—a fantastic *idea*"; or when a secondary school teacher recounts to his pupils the history of the European Middle Ages and the rise and fall of the Church's power, in order to let them draw their own parallels; or when a film director uses the color black—the rulers' favorite—as the color of death. Like termites, they are slowly but surely hollowing out the Islamic Republic's rigid edifice of rules, leaving the shell intact—but so thin that you can already see the reality glimmering through.

These sorts of private rebellions and indirect, veiled criticisms have been complemented in the last few years by unprecedented and increasingly frequent public manifestations of disaffection with the regime, arising for the most part from Iran's colleges and universities, and especially from the student movement (which, ironically, had been in the vanguard of the Khomeini revolution). These rebels were raised with the language of martyrdom, and have learned to use it against their rulers. When, for example, the ruling clerics sentenced to death a dissident history professor, Haschem Aghadschari, for alleged blasphemy in November 2002, he steadfastly refused to appeal the verdict in the biased court system and declared his willingness to "die as a martyr." Recognizing that their own language of martyrdom was being thrown back at them, the clerical-dominated judiciary backtracked of its own accord and revoked the sentence. The same official restraint was at work in the government's treatment of student protests against the Aghadschari sentence. Whereas two years previously the police had joined in an orgy of beatings of student protesters in their dormitories, this time they put away their helmets, shields and truncheons and politely asked the students if they wouldn't mind going home.[4] The worst thing that could have happened for the government would have been a dead student—for in Iran, he whose blood is shed in defeat dies as a martyr and is seen as a victor.

But the coalition of the mullahs, wealthy oligarchs, and military elite that rule Iran shows no signs of disintegrating in the face of these setbacks, and indeed has too much to lose to go without a struggle. This much is clear from the fierce repression of recent student demonstrations, and the harassment, imprisonment, and torture of student leaders begun in the summer of 2003. It is this powerful coalition of the status quo, forming a veritable state within the state and subject to no popular or legal control whatsoever, which is responsible for maintaining Iran's officially antagonistic stance towards the West, and specifically towards Khomeini's "Great Satan," the United States. Iran's hard-line ruling clerics have every reason to foster suspicions that Iran is carrying out a secret atomic weapons program, granting shelter to America's archenemies, the al-Qaeda fighters, and financing Islamic militants the world over, including Hamas.

Iran's ruling mullahs were given a huge boost by President Bush's now famous State of the Union address to the U.S. Congress in January 2002, in which he lumped Iran together with Iraq and North Korea in an "axis of evil." The speech placed Iran's reformist president Khatami, who had been cautiously attempting a *rapprochement* with the Americans, on the defensive, forcing him to join with his rivals, the conservative mullahs in Iran's authoritarian judiciary, in a public reiteration of the old anti-American position. Apart from its undermining of Khatami reformists, what made Bush's stigmatization of Iran in the "axis of evil" speech so unnecessary and inflammatory was the lack of objective proof that the current Iranian regime is engaged in the sort of mischief the Bush administration is accusing it of. There has never been any indication, for example, of pre– or post–September 11 Iranian support for the former Taliban regime in Afghanistan. The Taliban never had any friends in Teheran; indeed, the Iranian regime deployed thousands of troops on its border with Afghanistan in 1998 after the Taliban admitted to having murdered eight Iranian diplomats and a journalist in Mazar-e Sharif, and relations further deteriorated with Taliban massacres of members of the Shi'ite minority in central Afghanistan during that same year. Iran supported the Northern Alliance of anti-Taliban militia groups years before the Americans showed any interest, and lost hundreds of soldiers in the battle against heroin smugglers tolerated by the Taliban regime. And in the post-Taliban era, Iran has stepped up to become one of the most important donor-nations in the struggle to reconstruct and stabilize that war-torn country. Iranian intervention has persuaded some of the more recalcitrant Afghan warlords to cooperate with the new Afghan president, Hamid Karzai. An "axis of evil"? This phrase, at best, accurately describes an alliance of hard-liners within Iran striving to block precisely what Khatami and, with him, the majority of Iranians want for their country (and what the Bush administration is also calling for): rule of law, restrictions on state power, women's rights, protection of property, free speech, justice, and religious tolerance.[5]

In the impoverished south end of Teheran, in a district filled with plain, two-story houses with tiny open yards, the Bahman Cultural Center looks like an inviting oasis in the desert. Its cheerful, bright grounds consist of lawns, park benches, fountains, a cinema and planetarium, lecture and concert halls, and a small children's library. Nedda, a bright, opinionated sixteen-year-old schoolgirl, is standing on the center's grounds and looks up, completely at a loss. On the wall of a house across from the center's children's library, which is named after a thirteen-year-old martyr who threw himself under an Iraqi tank while detonating a hand grenade in 1982, there is a painting depicting seven young would-be martyrs sporting headbands that signal their willingness to die. They await a sign from the ghostly, other-worldly face of Khomeini, which appears in the corner. "I don't understand how anyone can be glad if one of their family or someone they love gets shot dead," says Nedda, shaking her head. "I was really sad when Grandpa died—and he was old."

The grotesque contradiction between the incitement to suicide martyrdom on the wall and the life-affirming atmosphere of the cultural center is hardly noticed in this community. Nedda has passed by that painting on her way to the center hundreds of times, but only began reflecting on its message after I reminded her of its existence. "All that stuff about the martyrs," says Nedda, shrugging her shoulders as if such stories have nothing to do with her. She had just been born when the young suicide bomber for whom the center is named blew himself up, and their biographies are worlds apart. "There was a war then— they told us about it at school." Quickly changing the subject to more interesting matters, Nedda, pulling her head-scarf back over her recalcitrant wisps of dark hair, expresses hope of being accepted into the center's orchestra. "I'd love to be a violinist. And playing here would be my only chance to get free lessons. We can't afford private ones."

✤

A still melancholy lies over the massive cemetery in the south end of Teheran, Behesht-e Zahra, built in the 1980s to honor those fallen during the Iran-Iraq War. The cemetery's adjacent halls, where martyr festivities took place at the height of the war, are still there, but as a bored caretaker assures me, "nobody uses them any more." "It's a pity, really," he continues, "but no sooner were the tents replaced by proper halls than the war stopped. People did keep coming for a while, but now they only bother going to the graves outside. Yes, they downright ignore this place."

I walked over to the gravesites to see if the young martyrs' graves were indeed being visited. Evidence of recent visits, in the form of freshly laid flowers on the weathered gravestones, were everywhere. A mother who has gone grey is standing in front of one of the little stone markers, quietly crying and, so it seems to me from a distance, conducting an imaginary conversation with her dead son. Initially uncomfortable as I approach her and disturb her private moment of grief, she is soon telling me about a terrible day in 1984, when her little boy Reza, then aged thirteen, came home from school and announced proudly that he was going to the front. She tells me of her helplessness and despair at that moment, knowing the futility of opposing a decision supported by her son's teachers, and by her own government—and knowing that no help would be forthcoming from her husband—who was at the front himself.

She then tells me about Reza's death, after five weeks at the front, and about the long years that followed it, when she repeatedly tried to persuade herself that it really had been a good and meaningful death. About how she turned, as she put it, "black" with pain and had to see a psychiatrist, about how it took her years to pluck up the courage to begin visiting Reza's grave regularly. About how she finally allowed herself to grieve for her son rather than struggle, against all natural feeling, to see her son's death as a worthwhile sacrifice for the Imam, and the Revolution, and as a gateway to Paradise. "I can't presume to judge," says Reza's mother with that indefatigable Iranian politeness. "But I don't believe it's God's will for someone to just throw his life away." Having said her piece, she stands up, gathers up her chador, and disappears, receding from view in the stony forest of gravestones.

Thus has Iran, whose religio-political leadership sent tens of thousands of young war volunteers to their deaths some twenty years ago, and whose charismatic revolutionary leader Khomeini drafted plans to export the Islamic Revolution abroad, turned away from the sort of extremism that fosters suicide bombing brigades. While its full membership in the community of civilized nations is still blocked by retrograde Khomeini nostalgia from within the power-wielding clergy, the process of enlightenment—a process, it must be stressed, that has taken its own path, without any American-sponsored regime change— is undeniable in Iranian society as a whole.

It is unlikely that the main sources of suicide bombing today—from the embattled Chechens to the Palestinians and the jihadist al-Qaeda— will be destroyed by sheer Western military might, however sophisticated, devastating, and well financed it may be. The Bin Ladens of the world actually feed off of massive military reprisals, which always involve Western (American) incursion into foreign territory, the support of local (and locally hated) despots, and a resulting local or nationalist backlash that the planners of terror can exploit and co-opt. We see it in American-occupied Iraq, in the almost daily bomb attacks directed at U.S. soldiers. Global manipulators of resentment and fear like Bin Laden can be defeated only from within, by their own societies and cultures. As the Syrian-born poet Adonis (Ali Ahmed Said) wrote in the immediate aftermath of September 11, "The war that must be fought is one that destroys, from the inside out, the reasons for a phenomenon such as Bin Laden. It must be a war for democracy, freedom, human rights—and for institutions that protect, defend and consolidate these values. . . . Only a war such as this—against oppression and injustice, against the disregard for human rights and international law, and against poverty and ignorance—can destroy terrorism, violence and barbarism and can contribute to preserving the dignity of human beings."[6]

Notes

※

Introduction
The Power of the Powerless

1. Stephen Frederic Dale, "Religious Suicide in Islamic Asia: Anticolonial Terrorism in India, Indonesia, and the Philippines," in *Journal of Conflict Resolution* 1998: 7–59.

2. Otto Krätz, "Der Mann, der Sprengstoff zähmte," *Süddeutsche Zeitung,* weekend supplement, September 2001, p. 1.

3. Arno Plack, "Vom Attentat direkt ins Paradies," *Die Weltwoche,* September 20, 2001, p. 20.

4. Jim Yardley, "Portrait of a Terrorist," *New York Times,* October 10, 2001.

5. "Road to September: A Careful Sequence of Mundane Dealings Sowed a Day of Terror," *Wall Street Journal,* October 16, 2001, p. A1.

6. Steven Hassan, psychologist and expert on sects, in *Psychologie Heute,* February 2002: 67.

7. Wolfgang Sofsky, *Zeiten des Schreckens. Amok, Terror, Krieg* (Frankfurt: Fischer, 2002), 181.

8. Harro Albrecht, Sabine Etzold, and Hans Schuh, "Attentäter wie du und ich," *Die Zeit,* September 19, 2001.

9. According to Ehud Sprinzak, the GIA, the "armed Islamic groups," carried out a suicide attack in the 1990s. However, nobody claimed responsibility, and it's also possible that it might have been an accident.

10. [Translator's note: this effect gets its name from Goethe's famous novel *Die Leiden des jungen Werthers* (*The Sorrows of Young Werther*), in which the eponymous "hero" commits suicide.]

Chapter 1
The Original Assassins

1. [Translator's note: the Abassids took their name from al-Abbas, a paternal uncle and early supporter of Muhammad, and held the caliphate from 749 until 1258 C.E.]

2. "Die anthropologische Wunde in unserer Beziehung zum Westen," in *Islam, Demokratie, Moderne. Aktuelle Antworten arabischer Denker,* ed. Erdmute Heller and Hassouna Mosbahi (Munich: C. H. Beck, 1998), 82.

3. To be more precise, we are referring to a sect within the Ismaelite or "Seven Shia" group that broke away from Shia Islam, a sect that recognizes seven rather than twelve legitimate followers of the Prophet and that is characterized by its marked receptivity to mystical and philosophical traditions as well as by its elitist secret doctrines. Among the latter-day descendants of this sect are the Druze (mainly in Syria, Israel, and Lebanon) and the Alawites (mainly in Syria).

4. Bernard Lewis, *The Assassins: A Radical Sect in Islam* (London: Weidenfeld and Nicolson, 1967), 28.

5. Ibid., 47.

6. Handed down by Rashid ad-Din and other medieval sources; quoted by Lewis, *The Assassins*, 47.

7. The sources that medieval European authors such as Marco Polo, Arnold of Lübeck, Benjamin of Tudela, or Denis Lebey de Batilly drew on were above all the polemics of Sunni authors who wrote *pro domo* and simply portrayed the assassins as the monstrous products of sin. Particularly conspicuous in this regard were Ibn Rizam and Akhu Muhsin, who even went so far as to accuse the assassins of "a secret conspiracy to abolish Islam." Cf. Farhad Daftery, *The Assassin Legends: Myth of the Isma'ilis* (London: J. B. Tauris, 1995).

8. The accusation that has been publicly disseminated, especially by U.S. government sources and the American media (for example by Ken Timmerman on August 11, 1998 in the *Wall Street Journal*), that Iran is to blame for all Islamic terrorist attacks, ignores the deeply rooted antagonism between Shia and Sunni radicals. Thus Iran's leadership and the Taliban were in no way allied to one another but were in fact mortal enemies, especially after the Taliban militia had murdered thousands of Shi'ites belonging to the Afghan people of Hazara. Anti-Shi'ite polemics such as the Friday sermons of Sheikh Huzaifi are constantly cropping up in books and newspapers in, for instance, Pakistan. Cf. Olivier Roy, "Die Sunnitische Internationale aus dem Niemandsland," *Le monde diplomatique,* October 16, 1998.

9. Fatima Mernissi, *Islam und Democratice: Die Angst vor der Moderne* (Freiberg: Herder, 2002), p. 102.

10. Hisham Djait, "Das arabisch-muslimische Denken und die Aufklärung," in *Islam, Demokratie, Moderne*, 31.

11. Shakib Arslan, *Limadha ta'khara al-muslimun wa limadha taqaddama ghairahum*, Cairo, 1930, quoted in Bassam Tibi, *Der Islam und das Problem der kulturellen Bewältigung sozialen Wandels* (Frankfurt: Suhrkamp, 1991), 160.

12. Muhammad b. 'Ali al-Shawkan, *Nayl al-Awtar Sharh Muntaqa al-Akhbar* (Cairo: Dar al-Hadith, n.d.), 7: 166.

13. *Der Islam und das Problem der kulturellen Bewältigung sozialen Wandels, 59.*

Chapter 2
A Key to Paradise around Their Necks

1. Heinz Halm, *Der Shiitische Islam* (Munich: C. H. Beck, 1994), 28.
2. Christopher Reuter, "Ein Gottesstaat wird menschlich," *Geo*, 2, 1999, p. 84.
3. Halm, *Der Shiitische Islam*, 46.
4. Wiebke Ghalandaran, *Die Mütter der Märtyrer. Der iranisch-irakische Krieg und seine Auswirkungen auf das Bild der Frau in der Ideologie der Islamischen Republik* (Bonn, Master's thesis, University of Bonn, 1997), 76.
5. Ghalandaran, *Die Mütter der Märtyrer*, 66.
6. Halm, *Der Shiitische Islam*, 155.
7. Karl-Heinrich Göbel, *Moderne Shiitische Politik und Staatsidee* (Opladen: Leske Verlag, 1984), 181.
8. Ghalandaran, *Die Mütter der Märtyrer*, 65.
9. Jan-Philipp Sendker, "Ich schikte 4,000 Kinder in den Tod," *Stern*, April 14, 1988.
10. *Stern*, March 24, 1983.
11. Ghalandaran, *Die Mütter der Märtyrer*, 72.
12. Ibid., 71.
13. Nirumand Bahmann, "Krieg, Krieg, bis zum Sieg," in *Bis die Gottlosen vernichtet sind* (Reinbeck, 1987), 95.
14. Sources: The Munzinger Archive, and an interview with a spokesman for the Bonyad Mostazafan and Janbazan Foundation, a giant mullah-controlled holding company that operates billions of dollars worth of assets confiscated from the late Shah, his family, and other elite Iranians. The Foundation provided for the medical care of the war wounded after the Iran-Iraq conflict, and became one of the most important sources of funding of the religiously conservative Teheran oligarchy.
15. Nirumand Bahman, "Khomeinis letztes Angebot," *Stern*, March 11, 1982.
16. Ibid., 89.
17. Ghalandaran, *Die Mütter der Märtyrer*, p. 13.

Chapter 3
The Marketing Strategists of Martyrdom

1. Robin Wright, *Sacred Rage: The Wrath of Militant Islam* (New York: Simon and Schuster, 1985), p. 72.
2. Ibid., 17.
3. Rolf Tophoven, *Sterben für Allah. Die Shi'iten und der Terrorismus* (Herford: Busse and Seewald, 1991), 134.
4. Thomas L. Friedman, *From Beirut to Jerusalem* (New York: Farrar Straus Giroux, 1989), 202.
5. Wright, *Sacred Rage*, 71.

6. [Translator's note: The Druze—a minority religious sect that broke away from Islam in the eleventh century—live mostly in Lebanon, Syria, Israel, and Jordan.]

7. Wright, *Sacred Rage,* 77.

8. Ibid., 84.

9. During one of several interviews conducted with him by the author.

10. Friedman, *From Beruit to Jerusalem,* 204.

11. Wright, *Sacred Rage,* 94.

12. Ibid., 82.

13. Cf. the very detailed assessment of various pieces of evidence in Magnus Ranstorp, *Hizb'allah in Lebanon: The Politics of the Western Hostage Crisis* (London: Palgrave Macmillan, 1996), 38 ff.

14. Addressees of an open letter from Hezbollah in 1985.

15. Tophoven, *Sterben für Allah,* 68.

16. Al-Manar TV, November 11, 1999. For political reasons, they only confessed to their involvement in early bombings years after they had taken place.

17. [Translator's note: *Umma* denotes the community of Muslims; the totality of all Muslims. It appears that in the early days of Islam, *umma* was used for the population of Mecca, but as Islam developed, it came to denote believers, and therefore excluded Meccans who had not converted.]

18. There are contradictory claims about when exactly the first Pasdaran arrived. Hala Jaber (in *Hezbollah,* New York: Columbia University Press, 1997, p. 20), Rolf Tophoven (*Sterben für Allah,* 68) and Stephan Rosiny (*Islamismus bei den Shiiten in Libanon,* Berlin, 1996, 353) say it was 1982; the Hezbollah chronicler Muhammad Abi Samra, on the other hand, claims that the first units had already arrived in the country in 1980 *(Al-Hayat,* June 26, 2000).

19. Interview with Fadlallah in the Hezbollah weekly paper *Al-Ahd,* November 14, 1996, quoted by Martin Kramer, "The Oracle of Hizbullah: Sayyid Muhammad Husayn Fadlallah," in *Spokesmen for the Despised: Fundamentalist Leaders of the Middle East,* ed. R. Scott Appleby (Chicago: University of Chicago Press, 1997), 129.

20. According to Reuven Paz, "The Islamic Legacy of Suicide Terrorism," in *Countering Suicide Terrorism: An International Conference* (Herzliya: Gefen Books, 2002), 3.

21. Author's interview with Timur Göksel, December, 2000.

22. Wright, *Sacred Rage,* 220.

23. Ibid.

24. Albrecht Metzger, *Der Himmel ist für Gott, der Staat für uns. Islamismus zwischen Gewalt und Demokratie* (Göttingen: Lamuv, 2000), 160.

25. Rosiny, *Islamismus bei den Shiiten in Libanon,* 67.

26. Quoted in Wright, *Sacred Rage,* 233.

27. Sheikh Hussein Fadlallah, Hezbollah spokesman Hussein Nabulsi, and Hezbollah "number two" Naim Qassem all confirm in interviews that the innovative tactic of having individual assassins loaded with explosives blow them-

selves up among their opponents, was essential in order to keep the number of their own casualties down.

28. From a speech by Ibrahim al-Amin, printed in the Hezbollah weekly paper *Al-Ahd,* January 23, 1997.

29. Jaber, *Hezbollah,* 86.

30. During a television broadcast on November 11, 1999 on Lebanese Al-Manar TV, commemorating the seventeenth anniversary of the first suicide bombing attack, a Hezbollah announcer mentioned that the attack had initially been scheduled for November 10, but had to be postponed until the 11th "due to unforeseen circumstances."

31. The term *shahid,* or martyr, is used by all Lebanese faiths for their men who die in battle; it's also used by Christians and even by secular groups. Cf. Rosiny, *Islamismus,* 233.

32. Regarding these terms, see Rosiny, *Islamismus,* 227 ff, and Jaber, *Hezbollah,* 81, as well as interviews with the Hezbollah spokesman, Muhammad Nabulsi, the Hezbollah cultural attaché Malek Wabdeh, and Muhammad Salam, the Lebanese journalist.

33. Jaber, *Hezbollah,* 26

34. Ibid., 161.

35. Ibid., 3.

36. Metzger, *Der Himmel is für Gott, der Staat für uns,* 67.

37. Interview conducted by my colleague in Berlin, Bernhard Hillekamp, for this book.

38. Amir Taheri, *Holy Terror: The Inside Story of Islamic Terrorism* (New York: Hutchinson Radins, 1987), 114.

39. The Israeli political scientist Yaron Ezrahi characterized the suicide attacks thus in an interview. See "Mit TNT in den Märtyrertod," http://www.secumag.de.

40. *The Daily Star,* Lebanese daily paper, September 14, 2001, and my own interview.

41. "How Respectable Is Hizbullah?" *The Economist,* December 1, 2001, 42.

42. Cf. Rosiny, *Islamismus bei den Shiiten in Libanon,* 181.

Chapter 4
Israel and Palestine

1. Author interview with Shlomo Gal, June 2001.

2. Author interview, June 2001.

3. Her name has been changed at her request.

4. These sums are remarkably low, and far from the famous $25,000 figure that the families were supposed to receive from Saddam Hussein. However, they reflect the experiences of the numerous families I visited while writing this book (though that does not, of course, exclude the possibility that other families received more).

5. A famous mother in Islamic and Arab history, who lost four sons in the war, but never lost her patience.

6. The standard diploma.

7. The honor of being a martyr.

8. Author interview with Yoram Schweitzer, researcher at the International Policy Institute for Counter-Terrorism (ICT, Herzliya), specializing in suicide bombing, September 2001.

9. Ethan Bronner, "Living With the Palestinian 'Catastrophe,'" *New York Times,* April 23, 1998.

10. Author interview with Graham Usher, the *Economist*'s Israel correspondent.

11. Neil MacFarquhar, "Blow for Blow: Israelis Demolish Bomb Maker's Family Home," *New York Times,* March 15, 1996.

12. Victor Kocher, "Palästinaas doppelgesichtige Islamisten," *Neue Zürcher Zeitung,* March 7, 1996.

13. MacFarquhar, "Blow for Blow."

14. Michael Lüders, "Bomben und Karitas," *Die Zeit,* September 12, 1997, 13.

15. Ibid.

16. Ibid.

17. Amanda Ripley, "Why Suicide Bombing is Now All the Rage," *Time,* April 15, 2002, p. 22.

18. Ibid.

19. Serge Schmemann, "Sheik Vows to Continue the Hamas Holy War against Israel," *New York Times,* October 23, 1997.

20. Cf. Shaul Mishal and Avraham Sela, *The Palestinian Hamas* (New York: Columbia University Press, 2000). The book's basic thesis concerns this multilayeredness: "Hamas is not a prisoner of its own dogmas" (vii).

21. Ibid.

22. MacFarquhar, "Blow for Blow."

23. "Mord mit Folgen," *Spiegel,* January 8, 1996, 115.

24. Ibid.

25. "Terror in Israel," *New York Times,* February 28, 1996.

26. Tilman Müller, "Bomben terror gegen den Tranm von Frieden," *Stern,* March 7, 1996, 146.

27. Serge Schmemann, "Bombing in Israel: Israeli Rage Rises as Bomb Kills 19, Imperiling Peace," *New York Times,* March 4, 1996.

28. Julian Ozanne, "Two Weeks of Terror Kill Peres's Hopes," *Financial Times,* March 5, 1996, 7.

29. *Tageszeitung,* October 6, 1997.

30. Schmemann, "Sheik Vows to Continue Hamas Holy War."

31. Inge Günther, "Geteile Freude über die Rückkehr des Scheichs Yassin," *Frankfurter Rundschau,* June 26, 1998, p. 2.

32. At the end of 2001, too, both were on fairly equal footing, being supported by about quarter of the population apiece.

33. Thorsten Schmitz, "Selbstmordattentat in Israel fordert mindestens sechs Tote," *Süddeutsche Zeitung,* May 19, 2001, 7.

34. Author interview with Ephraim Kam.

35. Lecture proceedings of the conference "Countering Suicide Terrorism," International Policy Institute for Counter-Terrorism (ICT, Herzliya, Israel), February 21–24, 2000.

36. *Ha'aretz,* June 4, 2001.

37. Lecture at the "Fighting Suicide Terrorism" Conference, Herzliya, Israel, quoted in *Ha'aretz,* December 19, 2001.

38. *Newsweek,* August 5, 2002.

39. Author interview with Yehuda Hiss, December 2001.

40. Nasra Hassan, "Letter from Gaza: An Arsenal of Believers," *The New Yorker,* December, 2001, p. 36.

41. Amos Oz, *Die Hugel des Libanon. Politische Essays* (Frankfurt, 1995), 202.

Chapter 5
Suicide or Martyrdom?

1. Al-Jazeera, September 12, 2001.

2. Al-Jazeera, October 12, 2001.

3. Al-Bukhari: *Nachrichten von Taten und Aussprüchen des Propheten Mohammed.* Selected, translated from the Arabic, and edited by Dieter Ferchl (Stuttgart: Reclam, 1991), 301 ff.

4. Markus Milwa, *Selbstmord in arabischen Gesellschaften* (master's thesis, University of Hamburg, 1999), 1.

5. *"Wala taqtuloo anfusakum inna Allaha kana bikum raheeman."*

6. "Auch tödtet euch nich selber! Denn Gott ist barmherzig," trans. Friedrich Rückert (1788–1866).

7. "Werdet keine Selbstmörder," German trans. Ludwig Ullman (1897); revised by Leo W. Winter in *Der Koran* (Berlin: W. Goldmann, 1959).

8. *Qur'an,* trans. Richard Bell (New York: Fortress Press, 1960; English translation originally published in 1937).

9. *Der Koran,* German trans. Max Henning (Stuttgart: Reclam, 1960).

10. *Der Koran,* trans. Radi Puret (Stuttgart: W. Kohlhammer, 1982). This is the translation most typically used in Germany.

11. Milwa, *Selbstmord,* 36.

12. Al-Bukhari, *Sahih,* collection of hadiths, edited by al-Imam az-Zubaidi (Riyadh, 1994), book 23 (burials), chapter 41, 340.

13. Milwa, *Selbstmord,* 40.

14. Franz Rosenthal, "On suicide in Islam," in *Journal of the American Oriental Society* 66 (1946): 245.

15. Milwa, *Selbstmord,* 25.

16. Ibid.

17. Cf. Walter Björkmann's article "Schahid," in *Enzyklopädie des Islam*, (Leipzig, 1934), IV: 279.

18. Author interview with Nizar Hamzeh, sociologist and Hezbollah expert, American University of Beirut, December 2000.

19. Hussein Muhammad Fadlallah, "Masa'il fighiya—intihar am shahada," in *Silsida nadwat al-hiwar al-usbu'iya bi Dimaschq* (Beirut, 1997), 730 ff.

20. These words were later published in *Ar-Raya* (Qatar daily newspaper), April 25, 2001.

21. *Al-Ahram al-Arabi*, (Cairo daily newspaper), February 3, 2001.

22. *Ash-Sharq Al-Awsat*, (Saudi daily paper, London), April 21, 2001.

23. *Al-Hayat al-Jahida*, (Palestinian daily paper, Ramallah), April 27, 2001.

24. *Al-Hayat*, (daily newspaper, London/Beirut), April 25, 2001.

25. *Al-Hayat*, April 25, 2001.

26. Ahmed al-Houny wrote about the "American fatwa" on April 24, 2001 in the daily paper *Al-Arab*. On the same day, the editorial of *Al-Quds al-Arabi*, also published in London, declared that "the true scholars are those whose fatwas condemn the Arab lack of support for those who sacrificed their blood for Al Aqsa" (i.e., the mosque, though this may also mean the Al Aqsa Intifada, or second Palestinian uprising unleashed in 2000).

27. Author interview with an Israeli security expert, who wished to remain anonymous.

28. *Saut al-Ama*, (Cairo), April 26, 2001.

29. *Al-Quds*, (Palestinian newspaper, Jerusalem), August 17, 1998.

30. Quoted from the Egyptian professor of law Taufiq ash-Shawi in *Al-Hayat*, April 27, 2001.

31. Ibid.

32. *Neue Zürcher Zeitung*, June 3, 2002 and Victor Kocher, "Geistlicher Support für Selbstmordattentäter," *Neue Zürcher Zeitung*, January 18–19, 2003, p. 9.

33. Kocher, "Geistlicher Support."

34. *Al-Istiqlal* (irregularly published newspaper of the Islamic Jihad, Gaza), August 20, 1999.

35. Yoram Feldner, "'72 Black Eyed Virgins': A Muslim Debate on the Rewards of Martyrs," published by MEMRI (Middle East Media Research Institute), *Inquiry and Analysis* Series, 74, October 30, 2001.

36. Surah ar-Rahman, verse 58.

37. Paul Nwyia, *Exégèse coranique et langage mystique* (Beirut, 1970), 103.

38. See the medieval Qur'anic commentator Al-Suyuti (1445–1505), quoted in Abdelwahab Bonhdiba, *La sexualité en Islam* (Paris: Presses Universitaries de France, 1975), 62.

39. Bayazid al-Bistami, died 874, quoted in Émile Dermenghem, *Vie des saints musulmans* (Paris: Seuil, 1983), 171.

40. Al-Bukhari, *Les Traditions Islamiques* (Paris: Adrien Maisonneuve, 1903–14), vol. II, 440.

41. Al-Suyuti in Bonhdiba, *La sexualite en Islam*, p. 94.

42. Ibid., p. 96; and see Mahmoud Tahmi, L'encyclopédisme musulman à l'âge classique: *Le livre de la création et de l'histoire de Maqdisi*. (Paris: Maisonneuve & Larose, 1998).

43. Susanne Knaul, "Die Märtyer," *Tageszeitung,* September 13, 2001, 9.

44. *Al-Istiqlal,* October 4, 2001.

45. *Ar-Risala,* August 16, 2001.

46. *Aacher Sa'a* (Egyptian weekly newspaper), May 9, 2001.

Chapter 6
Bushido Replaces *Allahu akbar*

1. Quoted from Klaus-Robert Heinemann, *Sturm der Götter* (Wiesbaden: Limes Verlag 1956, 67 ff.)—the German translation of a Tokyo University Press volume of farewell letters written by kamikaze pilots.

2. Other estimates speak of 4,000 to 5,000 such pilots.

3. Edwin Palmer Hoyt, *The Kamikazes* (New York: Arbor House 1983), 11.

4. Ibid., 23.

5. Klaus Scherer, *Kamikaze. Todesbefehl für Japans Jugend* (Munich: Iudicium 2001), 117 ff.

6. "Kamikaze-Pilot Atta" (*Süddeutsche Zeitung,* September 11, 2001); "Kamikaze-Netzwerk vom 11. September" (*Die Zeit,* October 3, 2001); "Kamikaze-Aktionen" (*Der Spiegel,*October 1, 2001); "Kamikaze-Terroristen" (*Die Woche,* November 2, 2001).

7. Saburo Ienaga, *Pacific War, Nineteen Thirty-One to Nineteen Forty-Five: A Critical Perspective on Japan's Role in World War II,* trans. Frank Baldwin (New York: Random House, 1978), 185.

8. It might be noted here that this classic samurai text emerged after an extended period of peace in Japan. The samurai Yamamoto Tsunetomo, on whose thoughts the book is based, lived in seclusion in a monastery and never fought in a battle.

9. Here as elsewhere, the dates relate to the period of reign.

10. A. J. Barker, *Suicide Weapon* (London: MacMillan, 1971), 111.

11. "Auf dem heiligen Winde reiten," *Neue Zürcher Zeitung,* August 23, 2001, 6.

12. Scherer, *Kanikaze,* 92.

13. Ibid., 51.

14. Robert Jay Lifton, *Destroying the World to Save It: Aum Shinrikyo, Apocalyptic Violence and the New Global Terrorism* (New York: Henry Holt, 2000), 285.

15. *Japan: Jahre des roten Terrors:* TV documentary by Michaël Prazan, broadcast on Arte (binational German-French state-funded channel), February 2, 2002.

16. Haruki Murakami, *Underground: The Tokyo Gas Attack and the Japanese Psyche* (New York: Vintage, 2001), 363.

Chapter 7
The Parasites of Anger

1. Reinhard Schulze, *Die Geschichte der islamischen Welt im 20. Jahrhundert* (Munich: C. H. Beck, 1994), 286.

2. Details come from Johannes Reissner's description of the occupation in *Orient* 21:2, (1980).

3. Phil Hirschkorn, Rohan Gunaratna, Ed Blanche, and Stefan Leader, "Special Report: Blowback," *Jane's Intelligence Review,* August 1, 2001, 14.

4. Olivier Roy, "Un fondamentalisme sunnite en panne de projet politique," *Le monde diplomatique,* October 16, 1998.

5. Cited by Rudolf Chimelli, "Großer Kopf einer hundertköpfizen Hydra," *Süddeutsche Zeitung,* September 17, 2001, 5.

6. Ibid.

7. On December 29, 1992 a bomb went off in a hotel in the Yemen port of Aden. It was supposed to hit American soldiers en route to Somalia, but missed them as they had already left. See Yonah Alexander and Michael S. Swetnam, *Usama Bin Laden's Al-Qaeda: Profile of a Terrorist Network* (New York: Transnational Publishers, 2001), 39.

8. Stefan Leader and Aaron Danis, "Tactical Insights from the Trial," *Jane's Intelligence Review,* August 1, 2001, 24.

9. *Jane's Intelligence Review,* April 1, 2000.

10. Michael Lüders, *Wir hungern nach dem Tod. Woher kommt die Gewalt im Dschihad-Islam?* (Hamburg: Arche Verlag, 2001), 104.

11. Evan Thompson and Sharon Squassoni, *Newsweek,* March 16, 2001, 30.

12. Karl Vick, "Cole Bombers Identified as Veterans of Afghan War," *International Herald Tribune,* November 17, 2002, 5.

13. Benjamin Weiser, "Terror Suspect Asked Officer to Kill Him, Interrogator Says." *New York Times,* October 19, 2000, 5.

14. John F. Burns, "F.B.I.'s Inquiry on Cole Attack Nearing a Halt," *New York Times,* August 21, 2001, A1.

15. Lüders, *Wir hungern nach dem Tod,* 105.

16. In September 2003, seven months after ordering American troops to invade and conquer Iraq, President Bush finally conceded in a press conference that "we've had no evidence that Saddam Hussein was involved with September 11th." Richard W. Stevenson, "A Change of Tone: Pitfalls Emerge in Iraq," *New York Times,* September 21, 2003.

17. "Deadly Attack Keeps World on Alert," *The Guardian,* September 4, 2002, 4.

18. Pepe Escobar, "Pakistan in the Shadow of Terror," *Asia Times,* August 28, 2002.

19. Interview with an al-Qaeda expert from a Western news agency.

20. Over the course of several weeks, I was able to conduct hours of interviews in the PUK's secret service prison in Sulaymaniyah. Interviewees included the pro-

fessed al-Qaeda cadre Kais Ibrahim Qadir; the former Iraqi secret service colleague Abderrahman ash-Shammari, who lived with Ansar for years; and two dispatched suicide bombers who were overcome by fear shortly before carrying out their mission and turned themselves in, but who didn't want to give their names.

21. Thomas Avenarius, *Süddeutsche Zeitung,* December 20, 2002, 3.

22. "18 Tote bei Selbstmordanschlag," *Frankfurter Allgemeine Zeitung,* June 6, 2003, 7.

23. "President Visits Arkansas," White House Press release, May 5, 2003.

24. "Mubarak: War in Iraq Will Create Increased Islamic Militancy," Associated Press wire story, March 31, 2003. This is exactly the line of argument adopted by Ayman al-Zawahiri, the number two man in the al-Qaeda hierarchy and its ideological head, in a series of essays collected in a recently published book that I discovered in April 2003, in a deserted toxin laboratory belonging to Ansar al-Islam in Iraqi Kurdistan. Ayman al-Zawahiri, *Loyalität und Vergeltung,* December 2002, place of publication unknown.

Chapter 8
Separatist Movements and Female Suicide Bombers

1. According to the 1996 report by the Special Investigation Team, the attack could be very quickly and more or less completely explained because the dead included a photographer who was supposed to take pictures of the attack for the LTTE. His camera survived the explosion and in the pictures taken moments before it happened, you can see the attackers and the other people involved.

2. Between 12 and 17 percent of Sri Lankan citizens belong to the Tamil ethnic group, including many who arrived in the country from India in the 19th century to work on the island's tea plantations.

3. Indira Lakshmanan, "The Face of Terror That Only Zealots See," *Boston Globe,* July 22, 2000.

4. Dr. Rohan Gunaratna, "Suicide Terrorism: A Global Threat," *Jane's Intelligence Review,* April 1, 2000.

5. Charu Lata Joshi, "Ultimate Sacrifice," *Far Eastern Economic Review,* June 1, 2000, 64.

6. "Fortschritte in Sri Lanka," *Frankfurter Allgemeine Zeitung,* February 8, 2002.

7. Narayan Swamy, M.R., *Tigers of Lanka: From Boys to Guerillas* (Delhi: Konark Publishers, 1994).

8. Indira Lakshmanan, "A Ruthless Tiger Leads Long Battle Against Sri Lanka," *The Boston Globe,* June 22, 2000; *Die Woche,* May 24, 1995.

9. Axel Tschentscher, *Deutsches Fallrecht* (Würzburg University, 1994).

10. Ibid.

11. Walter Keller, "Der gute Tamil in Berlin," in *Tageszeitung,* March 14, 2001.

12. According to a report by the "University Teachers for Human Rights in Jaffna," dated July 14, 2000, dissidents are tortured and executed.

13. Report by the "University Teachers for Human Rights in Jaffna," July 14, 2000.

14. According to Tim McGirk, "Tigerinnen töten leise," *Die Woche,* May 24, 1995.

15. *The Hindu* (Indian national daily newspaper), June 4, 1986.

16. McGirk, "Tigerinnen Töten leise," *Die Woche,* May 24, 1995.

17. The bodies of the Hindus are in such cases not burned, as the graves, decked out in all their bright colors, keep the memory of the fallen heroes more graphically alive.

18. *Patterns of Global Terrorism 2000,* United States Department of State, Office of the Coordinator for Counterterrorism, April 30, 2001.

19. Walter Keller and Michaela Told, *Tamilinnen in Sri Lanka. Frauen in Konfliktsituationen. Kurzstudie für schweizerische Flüchtlingshilfe* (Dortmund: SFH-Infobörse Nr 5/97, 1997).

20. International shipping is severely restricted for security reasons.

21. Raymond Bonner, "Tamil Guerrillas in Sri Lanka: Deadly and Armed to the Teeth," in *New York Times,* March 7, 1998.

22. Mostly from exile communities in the United States, Canada, Great Britain, France, Germany, the Netherlands, Italy, Scandinavia, Australia and South Africa.

23. Bonner, "Tamil Guerrillas in Sri Lanka."

24. Amy Waldman, "Masters of Suicide Bombing: Tamil Guerillas of Sri Lanka," *New York Times,* January 14, 2003, A7.

25. Quoted in Bernt Jonsson, "Sri Lanka's People Long for Peace," *WCC Feature* (Geneva: World Council of Churches Office of Communication), June 5, 2001.

26. From Velupillai Prabhakaran's speech of November 25, 2001 for the heroes' remembrance day.

27. Dogu Ergil, "Suicide Terrorism in Turkey: The Workers' Party of Kurdistan," lecture at the conference "Countering Suicide Terrorism," International Policy Institute for Counterterrorism (ICT), Herzliya, Israel, February 2000.

28. From the very beginning of LTTE-sponsored suicide attacks until February 2000, 30 to 40 percent of all Tamil LTTE attacks were committed by women. In the case of the PKK, it was 11 out of 15, and three out of six would-be suicide bombers foiled at the last moment were women. In Lebanon in the 1980s, women committed five of a total of the 12 or so suicide attacks attributed to the secular S.S.N.P. (Syrian Socialist Nationalist Party). Source: Yoram Schweitzer, "Suicide Terrorism: Development and Characteristics," (Herzliya: the International Policy Institute for Counter-Terrorism, April 21, 2000). The figures and factual information about the attacks in Turkey come, unless otherwise indicated, from the following studies: Taner Tavas, *Terorizm Baglaminda Intihar Saldirilari* (University of Ankara, 1999); Necati Alkan and Kemal Karademir, *Teror Orguitlerinin Intihar Eylemlerindeki Psikodinamik Gercekler* (Ankara, 1997).

29. In 2002, as part of its attempted self reinvention as a more mainstream political entity, the PKK officially changed its name to the Congress for Freedom and Democracy in Kurdistan (KADEK). The move, however, has been dismissed as a sham by Turkish authorities, and the organization remains on the European Union's official list of terrorist groups.

Chapter 9
After Martyrdom

1. Interview with Soroush, Teheran, November, 1998. See also Abdolkarim Soroush, *Reason, Freedom and Democracy in Islam,* ed. Mahmoud Sadri and Ahmad Sadri (New York: Oxford University Press, 2002).

2. Erich Follath, "Der verfluchte Gottesstaat," *Der Spiegel,* 44, 2001, p. 158.

3. Interview with Navid Kermani, May 2001.

4. Christiane Hoffman, "Beleidigte Baditschi," *Frankfurter Allgemeine Zeitung,* November 22, 2002.

5. "How Not to Make a Friend." *Economist,* February 9, 2002, 35.

6. Adonis, "Der Araber und der Andere," in *Die Zeit,* November 29, 2001. p. 40.

Index